Wedding Planning Checklist

THE FOLLOWING WEDDING PLANNING CHECKLIST ITEMIZES EVERYTHING you need to do or consider when planning your wedding and the best time frame in which to accomplish each activity.

This checklist assumes that you have at least nine months to plan your wedding. If your wedding is in less than nine months, just start at the beginning of the list and try to catch up as quickly as you can!

Use the boxes to the left of the items to check off the activities as you accomplish them. This will enable you to see your progress and help you determine what has been done and what still needs to be done.

NINE MONTHS & EARLIER

- ❏ Announce your engagement.
- ❏ Select a date for your wedding.
- ❏ Hire a professional wedding consultant.
- ❏ Select and reserve reception site.
- ❏ Determine the type of wedding you want: location, formality, time of day, number of guests.
- ❏ Determine budget and

- ❏ Develop a record-keeping system for payments made.
- ❏ Determine color scheme.
- ❏ Select a_ bridal g_ headpi_
- ❏ Select _ cerem_
- ❏ Decide if you want to include children among guests.
- ❏ Select and reserve your

- ❏ Consolidate all guest lists: bride's, groom's, bride's family, groom's family, and organize:
  1) must be invited
  2) should be invited
  _ to invite
  _ement notice
  _ograph
  _al newspaper.
  _ book
  _pher.
- ❏ Select maid of honor, best man, bridesmaids, and ushers.

SIX TO EIGHT WEEKS BEFORE WEDDING

- ❑ Mail invitations. Include accommodation choices and a map to assist guests in finding the ceremony and reception sites.

- ❑ Maintain a record of RSVPs and all gifts received. Send thank-you notes upon receipt of gifts.

- ❑ Determine hairstyle and makeup.

- ❑ Schedule to have your hair, makeup, and nails done the day of the wedding.

- ❑ Finalize shopping for wedding day accessories such as toasting glasses, ring pillow, etc.

- ❑ Obtain marriage license.

- ❑ Set up an area or a table in your home to display gifts as you receive them.

- ❑ Have your formal bridal portrait taken.

- ❑ Check with your local newspapers for wedding announcement requirements.

- ❑ Mail invitations to rehearsal dinner.

- ❑ Get blood test and health certificate.

- ❑ Send wedding announcement and photograph to your local newspapers.

- ❑ Select and reserve wedding attire for groom, ushers, ring bearer, and father of the bride.

- ❑ Check requirements to change your name and address on your driver's license, social security card, insurance policies, subscriptions, etc.

- ❑ Find "something old, something new, something borrowed, something blue, and a sixpence (shiny penny) for your shoe."

- ❑ Plan a luncheon or dinner with your bridesmaids. Give them their gifts at that time or at the rehearsal dinner.

- ❑ Select a guest book attendant. Decide where and when to have guests sign in.

- ❑ Finalize your menu, beverage, and alcohol order.

TWO TO SIX WEEKS BEFORE WEDDING

- ❑ Confirm ceremony details with your officiant.

- ❑ Arrange final fitting of bridesmaids' dresses.

- ❑ Have final fitting of your gown and headpiece.

- ❑ Make final floral selections.

- ❑ Finalize rehearsal dinner plans; arrange seating and write names on place cards, if desired.

- ❑ Make a detailed timeline for your wedding party.

- ❑ Make a detailed timeline for your service providers.

- ❑ Confirm details with all service providers, includ-

- ❑ Start packing for your honeymoon.

- ❑ Finalize addressing and stamping announcements.

- ❑ Meet with photographer and confirm special photos you want taken.

- ❑ Decide if you want to form a receiving line. If so, determine when and where to form the line.

- ❑ Contact guests who haven't responded.

- ❑ Meet with videographer and confirm special events or people you want videotaped.

- ❑ Pick up rings and check for fit

- ❑ Meet with musicians and confirm music to be played during special events such as the first dance.

- ❑ Remind bridesmaids and ushers of when and where to pick up their wedding attire.

- ❑ Purchase the lipstick, nail polish, and any other accessories you want your bridesmaids to wear.

- ❑ Determine ceremony seating for special guests. Give a list to the ushers.

- ❑ Plan reception room layout with your reception site manager or caterer. Write names

ing attire. Give them copies of your wedding timeline.

☐ Continue writing thank-you notes as gifts arrive.

place cards.

THE LAST WEEK

☐ Finish packing your suit cases for the honeymoon.

☐ Familiarize yourself with guests' names.

☐ Notify the post office to hold mail while you are away on your honeymoon.

☐ Arrange for someone to drive the getaway car.

☐ Review the schedule of events and last minute arrangements with your service providers.

☐ Give them each a detailed timeline and traveler's checks.

☐ Pick up wedding attire and make sure everything fits.

☐ Do final guest count and notify your caterer or reception site manager.

☐ Confirm all honeymoon reservations and accommodations. Pick up tickets

THE REHEARSAL DAY

☐ Arrange for someone to mail announcements the day after the wedding.

☐ Provide each member of your wedding party with a detailed schedule of events/timelines for the wedding day.

☐ Put suitcases in getaway car.

☐ Arrange for someone to return rental items such as tuxedos, slip, and cake pillars after the wedding.

☐ Arrange for someone to bring accessories such as flower basket, ring pillow, guest book and pen, toasting glasses, cake cutting knife, and napkins to the ceremony and reception.

☐ Give your bridesmaids the lipstick, nail polish, and accessories you want them to wear for the wedding.

☐ Give best man the officiant's fee and any other checks for service providers. Instruct him to deliver these checks the day of the wedding.

☐ Review ceremony seating with ushers.

THE WEDDING DAY

☐ Relax and enjoy your wedding!

☐ Simply follow your detailed schedule of events.

☐ Give the groom's ring to the maid of honor.

☐ Give the bride's ring to the best man.

May your wedding be beautiful, memorable & unique!

☐ officiant.

☐ Use the calendar provided to note all important activities: showers, luncheons, parties, get-togethers, etc.

☐ Order passport, visa, or birth certificate, if needed, for your honeymoon or marriage license.

☐ If ceremony or reception is at home, arrange for home or garden improvements as needed.

How expenses will be shared.

SIX TO NINE MONTHS BEFORE WEDDING

☐ Select and book ceremony musicians.

☐ Select and book reception musicians or DJ.

☐ Select and book videographer.

☐ Select and book florist.

☐ Select and book caterer, if needed.

☐ Schedule fittings and delivery dates for yourself, attendants, and flower girl.

☐ Select flower girl and ring bearer.

☐ Reserve wedding night bridal suite.

☐ Select attendants' dresses, shoes, and accessories.

FOUR TO SIX MONTHS BEFORE WEDDING

☐ Select and book all miscellaneous services, i.e., gift attendant, valet parking, etc.

☐ Purchase shoes and accessories.

☐ Begin to break in your shoes.

☐ Select and order wedding invitations, announcements, and other stationery such as thank-you notes, wedding programs, and seating cards.

☐ Arrange accommodations for out-of-town guests.

☐ Start planning your honeymoon.

☐ Register for gifts.

☐ Start shopping for each other's wedding gifts.

☐ Reserve rental items needed for ceremony.

☐ Finalize guest list.

☐ Address invitations or hire a calligrapher.

☐ Set date, time, and location for your rehearsal dinner.

TWO TO FOUR MONTHS BEFORE WEDDING

☐ Purchase gifts for wedding attendants.

☐ Consider writing a will and or a prenuptial agreement.

☐ Plan activities for guests both before and after the wedding.

☐ Select and book transportation for wedding day.

☐ Check blood test and marriage license requirements.

☐ Shop for wedding rings and have them engraved.

☐ Consider having your teeth cleaned or bleached.

☐ Select bakery and order wedding cake.

☐ Order party favors.

☐ Select and order room decorations.

☐ Purchase honeymoon attire and luggage.

EASY WEDDING
PLANNING NOTEBOOK

From
WedSpace.com
the Fastest Growing Bridal Community
and Wedding Planning Website

Written by
America's Top Wedding Experts
Alex & Elizabeth Lluch
Authors of Over 30 Best-Selling Wedding Books

WS Publishing Group
www.WSPublishingGroup.com
San Diego, California 92119

Easy Wedding Planning Notebook

By Alex & Elizabeth Lluch,
America's Top Wedding Experts

Published by WS Publishing Group
San Diego, California 92119
© Copyright 2010 by WS Publishing Group

Image Credits:
Front cover photo, Karen French
www.karenfrenchphotography.com
Phone: 714.968.5139
Email: info@karenfrenchphotography.com

For Inquiries:
Visit www.WSPublishingGroup.com
E-mail: info@WSPublishingGroup.com

Printed in China

ISBN 13: 978-1-936061-13-6

TABLE OF CONTENTS

GETTING STARTED

KAREN FRENCH

ENGAGEMENT PARTY DATE: _____

Engagement Party Time: _____

Engagement Party Location: _____

Contact Person: _____ Phone Number: _____

Website: _____ E-mail: _____

Notes: _____

BRIDAL SHOWER DATE: _____

Bridal Shower Time: _____

Bridal Shower Location: _____

Contact Person: _____ Phone Number: _____

Website: _____ E-mail: _____

Notes: _____

BACHELOR PARTY DATE: _____

Bachelor Party Time: _____

Bachelor Party Location: _____

Contact Person: _____ Phone Number: _____

Website: _____ E-mail: _____

Notes: _____

BACHELORETTE PARTY DATE: _____

Bachelorette Party Time: _____

Bachelorette Party Location: _____

Contact Person: _____ Phone Number: _____

Website: _____ E-mail: _____

Notes: _____

WEDDING EVENTS AT A GLANCE

CEREMONY REHEARSAL DATE: _____

Ceremony Rehearsal Time: _____

Ceremony Rehearsal Location: _____

Contact Person: _____   Phone Number: _____

Website: _____   E-mail: _____

Notes: _____

REHEARSAL DINNER DATE: _____

Rehearsal Dinner Time: _____

Rehearsal Dinner Location: _____

Contact Person: _____   Phone Number: _____

Website: _____   E-mail: _____

Notes: _____

CEREMONY DATE: _____

Ceremony Time: _____

Ceremony Location: _____

Contact Person: _____   Phone Number: _____

Website: _____   E-mail: _____

Notes: _____

RECEPTION DATE: _____

Reception Time: _____

Reception Location: _____

Contact Person: _____   Phone Number: _____

Website: _____   E-mail: _____

Notes: _____

VENDOR	COMPANY	CONTACT PERSON	PHONE #	WEBSITE/ E-MAIL
Wedding Consultant				
Ceremony Site				
Officiant				
Reception Site				
Caterer				
Liquor Services				
Wedding Gown				
Tuxedo Rental				
Photographer				
Videographer				
Stationer				
Calligrapher				
Music: Ceremony				

SERVICE PROVIDERS AT A GLANCE

VENDOR	COMPANY	CONTACT PERSON	PHONE #	WEBSITE/ E-MAIL
Music: Reception				
Florist				
Bakery				
Decorations				
Ice Sculpture				
Party Favors				
Balloonist				
Transportation				
Rental & Supplies				
Gift Suppliers				
Valet Services				
Gift Attendant				
Rehearsal Dinner				

BUDGET ANALYSIS CHECKLIST

Items in italics are traditionally paid for by the groom or his family.

CEREMONY

- ❏ Ceremony Site Fee
- ❏ *Officiant's Fee*
- ❏ *Officiant's Gratuity*
- ❏ Guest Book/Pen/Penholder
- ❏ Ring Bearer Pillow
- ❏ Flower Girl Basket

WEDDING ATTIRE

- ❏ Bridal Gown
- ❏ Alterations
- ❏ Headpiece/Veil
- ❏ Gloves
- ❏ Jewelry
- ❏ Garter/Stockings
- ❏ Shoes
- ❏ Hairdresser
- ❏ Makeup Artist
- ❏ Manicure/Pedicure
- ❏ *Groom's Formal Wear*

PHOTOGRAPHY

- ❏ Bride & Groom's Album
- ❏ Parents' Album
- ❏ Extra Prints
- ❏ Proofs/Previews
- ❏ Negatives/Digital Files
- ❏ Engagement Photograph
- ❏ Formal Bridal Portrait

VIDEOGRAPHY

- ❏ Main Video
- ❏ Titles
- ❏ Extra Hours
- ❏ Photo Montage
- ❏ Extra Copies

STATIONERY

- ❏ Invitations
- ❏ Response Cards
- ❏ Reception Cards
- ❏ Ceremony Cards
- ❏ Pew Cards
- ❏ Seating/Place Cards
- ❏ Rain Cards
- ❏ Maps
- ❏ Ceremony Programs
- ❏ Announcements
- ❏ Thank-You Notes
- ❏ Stamps
- ❏ Calligraphy
- ❏ Napkins/Matchbooks

RECEPTION

- ❏ Reception Site Fee
- ❏ Hors d'Oeuvres
- ❏ Main Meal/Caterer
- ❏ Liquor/Beverages
- ❏ Bartending/Bar Setup Fee

RECEPTION (CONT.)

- ❏ Corkage Fee
- ❏ Fee to Pour Coffee
- ❏ Service Providers' Meals
- ❏ Gratuity
- ❏ Party Favors
- ❏ Disposable Cameras
- ❏ Rose Petals/Rice
- ❏ Gift Attendant
- ❏ Parking Fee/Valet Services

MUSIC

- ❏ Ceremony Music
- ❏ Reception Music

BAKERY

- ❏ Wedding Cake
- ❏ *Groom's Cake*
- ❏ Cake Delivery/Setup Fee
- ❏ Cake-Cutting Fee
- ❏ Cake Top
- ❏ Cake Knife/Toasting Glasses

FLOWERS: BOUQUETS

- ❏ *Bride*
- ❏ Tossing
- ❏ Maid of Honor
- ❏ Bridesmaids

BUDGET ANALYSIS CHECKLIST

Items in italics are traditionally paid for by the groom or his family.

FLORAL HAIRPIECES

- ❑ Maid of Honor/ Bridesmaids
- ❑ Flower Girl

CORSAGES

- ❑ *Bride's Going Away*
- ❑ *Family Members*

BOUTONNIERES

- ❑ *Groom*
- ❑ *Ushers/Other Family Members*

CEREMONY SITE

- ❑ Main Altar
- ❑ Altar Candelabra
- ❑ Aisle Pews

RECEPTION SITE

- ❑ Head Table
- ❑ Guest Tables
- ❑ Buffet Table
- ❑ Punch Table
- ❑ Cake Table
- ❑ Cake
- ❑ Cake Knife
- ❑ Toasting Glasses
- ❑ Floral Delivery/Setup Fee

DECORATIONS

- ❑ Table Centerpieces
- ❑ Balloons

RENTAL ITEMS

- ❑ Bridal Slip
- ❑ Ceremony Accessories
- ❑ Tent/Canopy
- ❑ Dance Floor
- ❑ Tables/Chairs
- ❑ Linen/Tableware
- ❑ Heaters
- ❑ Lanterns
- ❑ Other Rental Items

GIFTS

- ❑ *Bride's Gift*
- ❑ Groom's Gift
- ❑ Bridesmaids' Gifts
- ❑ *Ushers' Gifts*

PARTIES

- ❑ Engagement Party
- ❑ Bridesmaids' Luncheon
- ❑ *Rehearsal Dinner*
- ❑ Bachelorette Party
- ❑ *Bachelor Party*

TRANSPORTATION

- ❑ Transportation

MISCELLANEOUS

- ❑ Newspaper Announcements
- ❑ *Marriage License*
- ❑ *Prenuptial Agreement*
- ❑ Bridal Gown Preservation
- ❑ Bridal Bouquet Preservation
- ❑ Wedding Consultant
- ❑ Wedding Planning Online
- ❑ Taxes

OTHER

- ❑ _____
- ❑ _____
- ❑ _____
- ❑ _____
- ❑ _____
- ❑ _____
- ❑ _____
- ❑ _____
- ❑ _____
- ❑ _____
- ❑ _____
- ❑ _____
- ❑ _____
- ❑ _____

BUDGET ANALYSIS WORKSHEET

Items in italics are traditionally paid for by the groom or his family.

WEDDING BUDGET	Budget	Actual
YOUR TOTAL WEDDING BUDGET	$	$
CEREMONY (Typically = 5% of Budget)	$	$
Ceremony Site Fee	$	$
Officiant's Fee	$	$
Officiant's Gratuity	$	$
Guest Book/Pen/Penholder	$	$
Ring Bearer Pillow	$	$
Flower Girl Basket	$	$
SUBTOTAL 1	$	$
WEDDING ATTIRE (Typically = 10% of Budget)	$	$
Bridal Gown	$	$
Alterations	$	$
Headpiece/Veil	$	$
Gloves	$	$
Jewelry	$	$
Garter/Stockings	$	$
Shoes	$	$
Hairdresser	$	$
Makeup Artist	$	$
Manicure/Pedicure	$	$
Groom's Formal Wear	$	$
SUBTOTAL 2	$	$
PHOTOGRAPHY (Typically = 9% of Budget)	$	$
Bride & Groom's Album	$	$
Parents' Album	$	$

WEDDING BUDGET	Budget	Actual
PHOTOGRAPHY (Cont.)	$	$
Extra Prints	$	$
Proofs/Previews	$	$
Negatives/Digital Files	$	$
Engagement Photograph	$	$
Formal Bridal Portrait	$	$
SUBTOTAL 3	$	$
VIDEOGRAPHY (Typically = 5% of Budget)	$	$
Main Video	$	$
Titles	$	$
Extra Hours	$	$
Photo Montage	$	$
Extra Copies	$	$
SUBTOTAL 4	$	$
STATIONERY (Typically = 4% of Budget)	$	$
Invitations	$	$
Response Cards	$	$
Reception Cards	$	$
Ceremony Cards	$	$
Pew Cards	$	$
Seating/Place Cards	$	$
Rain Cards	$	$
Maps	$	$
Ceremony Programs	$	$
Announcements	$	$
Thank-You Notes	$	$
Stamps	$	$
Calligraphy	$	$

BUDGET ANALYSIS WORKSHEET

WEDDING BUDGET	Budget	Actual	WEDDING BUDGET	Budget	Actual
STATIONERY (Cont.)	$	$	**BAKERY** (Cont.)	$	$
Napkins/Matchbooks	$	$	Cake-Cutting Fee	$	$
SUBTOTAL 5	$	$	Cake Top	$	$
			Cake Knife/Toasting Glasses	$	$
RECEPTION (Typically = 35% of Budget)	$	$	**SUBTOTAL 8**	$	$
Reception Site Fee	$	$	**FLOWERS** (Typically = 6% of Budget)	$	$
Hors d'Oeuvres	$	$			
Main Meal/Caterer	$	$	BOUQUETS	$	$
Liquor/Beverages	$	$	*Bride*	$	$
Bartending/Bar Setup Fee	$	$	Tossing	$	$
Corkage Fee	$	$	Maid of Honor	$	$
Fee to Pour Coffee	$	$	Bridesmaids	$	$
Service Providers' Meals	$	$	FLORAL HAIRPIECES	$	$
Gratuity	$	$	Maid of Honor/Brides-maids	$	$
Party Favors	$	$	Flower Girl	$	$
Disposable Cameras	$	$	CORSAGES	$	$
Rose Petals/Rice	$	$	*Bride's Going Away*	$	$
Gift Attendant	$	$	*Family Members*	$	$
Parking Fee/Valet Services	$	$	BOUTONNIERES	$	$
SUBTOTAL 6	$	$	*Groom*	$	$
			Ushers/Other Family Members	$	$
MUSIC (Typically = 5% of Budget)	$	$	CEREMONY SITE FLOWERS	$	$
Ceremony Music	$	$	Main Altar	$	$
Reception Music	$	$	Altar Candelabra	$	$
SUBTOTAL 7	$	$	Aisle Pews	$	$
			Reception Site	$	$
BAKERY (Typically = 2% of Budget)	$	$	RECEPTION SITE FLOWERS	$	$
Wedding Cake	$	$	Reception Site	$	$
Groom's Cake	$	$	Head Table	$	$
Cake Delivery/Setup Fee	$	$	Guest Tables	$	$

BUDGET ANALYSIS WORKSHEET

WEDDING BUDGET	Budget	Actual	WEDDING BUDGET	Budget	Actual
FLOWERS (Cont.)	$	$	**GIFTS** (Typically = 3% of Budget)	$	$
Buffet Table	$	$	*Bride's Gift*	$	$
Punch Table	$	$	Groom's Gift	$	$
Cake Table	$	$	Bridesmaids' Gifts	$	$
Cake	$	$	*Ushers' Gifts*	$	$
Cake Knife	$	$	**SUBTOTAL 13**	$	$
Toasting Glasses	$	$			
Floral Delivery/Setup Fee	$	$	**PARTIES** (Typically = 4% of Budget)	$	$
SUBTOTAL 9	$	$	Engagement Party	$	$
			Bridesmaids' Luncheon	$	$
DECORATIONS (Typically = 3% of Budget)	$	$	*Rehearsal Dinner*	$	$
Table Centerpieces	$	$	Bachelorette Party	$	$
Balloons	$	$	*Bachelor Party*	$	$
SUBTOTAL 10	$	$	**SUBTOTAL 14**	$	$
TRANSPORTATION (Typically = 2% of Budget)	$	$	**MISCELLANEOUS** (Typically = 4% of Budget)	$	$
Transportation	$	$	Newspaper Announcements	$	$
SUBTOTAL 11	$	$	*Marriage License*	$	$
			Prenuptial Agreement	$	$
RENTAL ITEMS (Typically = 3% of Budget)	$	$	Bridal Gown Preservation	$	$
Bridal Slip	$	$	Bridal Bouquet Preservation	$	$
Ceremony Accessories	$	$	Wedding Consultant	$	$
Tent/Canopy	$	$	Wedding Planning Online	$	$
Dance Floor	$	$	Taxes	$	$
Tables/Chairs	$	$	**SUBTOTAL 15**	$	$
Linen/Tableware	$	$			
Heaters	$	$	**GRAND TOTAL** (Add "Budget" & "Actual" Subtotals 1-15)	$	$
Lanterns	$	$			
Other Rental Items	$	$			
SUBTOTAL 12	$	$			

NOTES

CEREMONY
& ATTIRE

❋ ❀ ❋

KAREN FRENCH

CEREMONY SITE COMPARISON CHART

QUESTIONS	POSSIBILITY 1	POSSIBILITY 2
What is the name of the ceremony site?		
What is the website and e-mail of the ceremony site?		
What is the address of the ceremony site?		
What is the name and phone number of my contact person?		
What dates and times are available?		
Do vows need to be approved?		
What is the ceremony site fee?		
What is the payment policy?		
What is the cancellation policy?		
Does the facility have liability insurance?		
What are the minimum/maximum number of guests allowed?		
What is the denomination, if any, of the facility?		
What restrictions are there with regards to religion?		
Is an officiant available? At what cost?		
Are outside officiants allowed?		
Are any musical instruments available for our use?		
If so, what is the fee?		

QUESTIONS	POSSIBILITY 3	POSSIBILITY 4
What is the name of the ceremony site?		
What is the website and e-mail of the ceremony site?		
What is the address of the ceremony site?		
What is the name and phone number of my contact person?		
What dates and times are available?		
Do vows need to be approved?		
What is the ceremony site fee?		
What is the payment policy?		
What is the cancellation policy?		
Does the facility have liability insurance?		
What are the minimum/maximum number of guests allowed?		
What is the denomination, if any, of the facility?		
What restrictions are there with regards to religion?		
Is an officiant available? At what cost?		
Are outside officiants allowed?		
Are any musical instruments available for our use?		
If so, what is the fee?		

QUESTIONS	POSSIBILITY 1	POSSIBILITY 2
What music restrictions are there, if any?		
What photography restrictions are there, if any?		
What videography restrictions are there, if any?		
Are there any restrictions for rice/petal-tossing?		
Are candlelight ceremonies allowed?		
What floral decorations are available/allowed?		
When is my rehearsal to be scheduled?		
Is there handicap accessibility and parking?		
How many parking spaces are available for my wedding party?		
Where are they located?		
How many parking spaces are available for my guests?		
What rental items are necessary?		
What is the fee?		

QUESTIONS	POSSIBILITY 3	POSSIBILITY 4
What music restrictions are there, if any?		
What photography restrictions are there, if any?		
What videography restrictions are there, if any?		
Are there any restrictions for rice/petal-tossing?		
Are candlelight ceremonies allowed?		
What floral decorations are available/allowed?		
When is my rehearsal to be scheduled?		
Is there handicap accessibility and parking?		
How many parking spaces are available for my wedding party?		
Where are they located?		
How many parking spaces are available for my guests?		
What rental items are necessary?		
What is the fee?		

CEREMONY READING SELECTIONS

SOURCE	SELECTION	READ BY	WHEN

PERSONALIZED VOWS

BRIDE'S VOWS: _____
_____
_____
_____
_____
_____
_____
_____
_____
_____
_____

GROOM'S VOWS: _____
_____
_____
_____
_____
_____
_____
_____
_____
_____

PERSONALIZED RING CEREMONY: _____
_____
_____
_____
_____
_____
_____

PEW SEATING ARRANGEMENTS

Complete this form only after finalizing your guest list.

BRIDE'S FAMILY SECTION

• PEW _____   • PEW _____   • PEW _____

_____   _____   _____
_____   _____   _____
_____   _____   _____
_____   _____   _____
_____   _____   _____
_____   _____   _____
_____   _____   _____
_____   _____   _____

• PEW _____   • PEW _____   • PEW _____

_____   _____   _____
_____   _____   _____
_____   _____   _____
_____   _____   _____
_____   _____   _____
_____   _____   _____
_____   _____   _____

• PEW _____   • PEW _____   • PEW _____

_____   _____   _____
_____   _____   _____
_____   _____   _____
_____   _____   _____
_____   _____   _____
_____   _____   _____

PEW SEATING ARRANGEMENTS

Complete this form only after finalizing your guest list.

GROOM'S FAMILY SECTION

• PEW _____   • PEW _____   • PEW _____

_____   _____   _____
_____   _____   _____
_____   _____   _____
_____   _____   _____
_____   _____   _____
_____   _____   _____
_____   _____   _____

• PEW _____   • PEW _____   • PEW _____

_____   _____   _____
_____   _____   _____
_____   _____   _____
_____   _____   _____
_____   _____   _____
_____   _____   _____
_____   _____   _____

• PEW _____   • PEW _____   • PEW _____

_____   _____   _____
_____   _____   _____
_____   _____   _____
_____   _____   _____
_____   _____   _____
_____   _____   _____

BRIDAL ATTIRE CHECKLIST

ITEM	DESCRIPTION	SOURCE
Full Slip		
Garter		
Gloves		
Gown		
Handbag		
Jewelry		
Lingerie		
Panty Hose		
Petticoat or Slip		
Shoes		
Something Old		
Something New		
Something Borrowed		
Something Blue		
Stocking		
Veil/Hat		
Other:		
Other:		
Other:		
Other:		

BRIDAL ATTIRE INFORMATION SHEET

BRIDAL ATTIRE

Bridal Boutique:

Date Ordered:

Salesperson: Phone Number:

Address:

City: State: Zip Code:

Website:

E-mail:

Description of Dress:

	MANUFACTURER	STYLE	SIZE	COST
Wedding Gown				
Headpiece				
Veil/Hat				
Shoes				

GOWN ALTERATIONS

Location:

Cost:

Tailor: Phone Number:

Address:

City: State: Zip Code:

Website:

E-mail:

	ALTERATION	DATE/TIME
First Alteration		
Second Alteration		
Third Alteration		
Final Alteration		

BRIDAL BOUTIQUE COMPARISON CHART

QUESTIONS	POSSIBILITY 1	POSSIBILITY 2
What is the name of the bridal boutique?		
What is the website and e-mail of the bridal boutique?		
What is the address of the bridal boutique?		
What is the name and phone number of my contact person?		
What are your hours of operation? Are appointments needed?		
Do you offer any discounts or giveaways?		
What major bridal gown lines do you carry?		
Do you carry outfits for the mother of the bride?		
Do you carry bridesmaids gowns and/or tuxedos?		
Do you carry outfits for the flower girl and ring bearer?		
What is the cost of the desired bridal gown?		
What is the cost of the desired headpiece?		
Do you offer in-house alterations? If so, what are your fees?		
Do you carry bridal shoes? What is their price range?		
Do you dye shoes to match outfits?		
Do you rent bridal slips? If so, what is the rental fee?		
What is the estimated date of delivery for my gown?		
What is your payment policy/cancellation policy?		

QUESTIONS	POSSIBILITY 3	POSSIBILITY 4
What is the name of the bridal boutique?		
What is the website and e-mail of the bridal boutique?		
What is the address of the bridal boutique?		
What is the name and phone number of my contact person?		
What are your hours of operation? Are appointments needed?		
Do you offer any discounts or giveaways?		
What major bridal gown lines do you carry?		
Do you carry outfits for the mother of the bride?		
Do you carry bridesmaids gowns and/or tuxedos?		
Do you carry outfits for the flower girl and ring bearer?		
What is the cost of the desired bridal gown?		
What is the cost of the desired headpiece?		
Do you offer in-house alterations? If so, what are your fees?		
Do you carry bridal shoes? What is their price range?		
Do you dye shoes to match outfits?		
Do you rent bridal slips? If so, what is the rental fee?		
What is the estimated date of delivery for my gown?		
What is your payment policy/cancellation policy?		

BRIDESMAIDS' ATTIRE INFORMATION SHEET

Make as many copies of this form as needed.

BRIDESMAIDS' ATTIRE

Bridal Boutique: _____

Date Ordered: _____

Salesperson: _____ Phone Number: _____

Address: _____

City: _____ State: _____ Zip Code: _____

Website: _____

E-mail: _____

Description of Dress: _____

Cost: _____

Manufacturer: _____

Date Ready: _____

BRIDESMAIDS' SIZES

NAME	DRESS	HEAD	WEIGHT	HEIGHT	WAIST	GLOVES	SHOES	HOSE

GROOM/GROOMSMEN'S ATTIRE
INFORMATION SHEET

Make as many copies of this form as needed.

GROOM/GROOMSMEN'S ATTIRE

Store Name: _____

Date Ordered: _____

Salesperson: _____ Phone Number: _____

Address: _____

City: _____ State: _____ Zip Code: _____

Website: _____

E-mail: _____

Description of Tuxedo: _____

Cost: _____

Manufacturer: _____

Date Ready: _____

GROOM/GROOMSMEN'S SIZES

NAME	HEIGHT	WEIGHT	WAIST	SLEEVE	INSEAM	JACKET	NECK	SHOES

BRIDAL BEAUTY INFORMATION SHEET

APPOINTMENT	DATE	TIME	LOCATION	NOTES
Hair Trial Run				
Makeup Trial Run				
Wedding Day Hair				
Wedding Day Makeup				
Bridesmaids' Hair				
Bridesmaids' Makeup				
Nail Salon				
Other:				
Other:				
Other:				

PHOTOGRAPHY & VIDEOGRAPHY

KAREN FRENCH

PHOTOGRAPHER COMPARISON CHART

QUESTIONS	POSSIBILITY 1	POSSIBILITY 2
What is the name and phone number of the photographer?		
What is the website and e-mail of the photographer?		
What is the address of the photographer?		
How many years of experience do you have as a photographer?		
What percentage of your business is dedicated to weddings?		
Approximately how many weddings have you photographed?		
Are you the person who will photograph my wedding?		
Will you bring an assistant with you to my wedding?		
How do you typically dress for weddings?		
Do you have a professional studio?		
What type of equipment do you use?		
Do you bring backup equipment with you to weddings?		
Do you need to visit the ceremony and reception sites prior to the wedding?		
Do you have liability insurance?		
Are you skilled in diffused lighting and soft focus?		
Can you take studio portraits?		
Can you retouch my images?		

PHOTOGRAPHER COMPARISON CHART (CONT.)

QUESTIONS	POSSIBILITY 3	POSSIBILITY 4
What is the name and phone number of the photographer?		
What is the website and e-mail of the photographer?		
What is the address of the photographer?		
How many years of experience do you have as a photographer?		
What percentage of your business is dedicated to weddings?		
Approximately how many weddings have you photographed?		
Are you the person who will photograph my wedding?		
Will you bring an assistant with you to my wedding?		
How do you typically dress for weddings?		
Do you have a professional studio?		
What type of equipment do you use?		
Do you bring backup equipment with you to weddings?		
Do you need to visit the ceremony and reception sites prior to the wedding?		
Do you have liability insurance?		
Are you skilled in diffused lighting and soft focus?		
Can you take studio portraits?		
Can you retouch my images?		

QUESTIONS	POSSIBILITY 1	POSSIBILITY 2
Can digital files be purchased? If so, what is the cost?		
What is the cost of the package I am interested in?		
What is your payment policy?		
What is your cancellation policy?		
Do you offer a money-back guarantee?		
Do you use paper proofs or DVD proofing?		
How many photographs will I have to choose from?		
When will I get my proofs?		
When will I get my album?		
What is the cost of an engagement portrait?		
What is the cost of a formal bridal portrait?		
What is the cost of a parent album?		
What is the cost of a 5 x 7 reprint?		
What is the cost of an 8 x 10 reprint?		
What is the cost of an 11 x 14 reprint?		
What is the cost per additional hour of shooting at the wedding?		

QUESTIONS	POSSIBILITY 3	POSSIBILITY 4
Can digital files be purchased? If so, what is the cost?		
What is the cost of the package I am interested in?		
What is your payment policy?		
What is your cancellation policy?		
Do you offer a money-back guarantee?		
Do you use paper proofs or DVD proofing?		
How many photographs will I have to choose from?		
When will I get my proofs?		
When will I get my album?		
What is the cost of an engagement portrait?		
What is the cost of a formal bridal portrait?		
What is the cost of a parent album?		
What is the cost of a 5 x 7 reprint?		
What is the cost of an 8 x 10 reprint?		
What is the cost of an 11 x 14 reprint?		
What is the cost per additional hour of shooting at the wedding?		

PHOTOGRAPHER'S INFORMATION

Once it is completed, make a copy of this form to give to your photographer as a reminder of your various events.

THE WEDDING OF: _____ Phone Number: _____

PHOTOGRAPHER'S COMPANY

Business Name: _____

Address: _____

City: _____ State: _____ Zip Code: _____

Website: _____ E-mail: _____

Photographer's Name: _____ Phone Number: _____

Assistant's Name: _____ Phone Number: _____

Notes: _____

ENGAGEMENT PHOTOS

Date: _____ Time: _____

Location: _____

Address: _____

City: _____ State: _____ Zip Code: _____

Notes: _____

BRIDAL PORTRAIT

Date: _____ Time: _____

Location: _____

Address: _____

City: _____ State: _____ Zip Code: _____

Notes: _____

PHOTOGRAPHER'S INFORMATION

Once it is completed, make a copy of this form to give to your photographer as a reminder of your various events.

OTHER EVENTS

Event:

Date: Time:

Location:

Address:

City: State: Zip Code:

Notes:

CEREMONY

Date: Arrival Time: Departure Time:

Location:

Address:

City: State: Zip Code:

Ceremony Restrictions/Guidelines:

Notes:

RECEPTION

Date: Arrival Time: Departure Time:

Location:

Address:

City: State: Zip Code:

Reception Restrictions/Guidelines:

Notes:

WEDDING PHOTOGRAPHS

Check off all photographs you would like taken throughout your wedding day.
Then make a copy of this form and give it to your photographer.

PRE-CEREMONY PHOTOGRAPHS

❑ Bride leaving her house

❑ Wedding rings with the invitation

❑ Bride getting dressed for the ceremony

❑ Bride looking at her bridal bouquet

❑ Maid of honor putting garter on bride's leg

❑ Bride by herself

❑ Bride with her mother

❑ Bride with her father

❑ Bride with mother and father

❑ Bride with her entire family and/or any combination thereof

❑ Bride with her maid of honor

❑ Bride with her bridesmaids

❑ Bride with the flower girl and/or ring bearer

❑ Bride's mother putting on her corsage

❑ Groom leaving his house

❑ Groom putting on his boutonniere

❑ Groom with his mother

❑ Groom with his father

❑ Groom with mother and father

❑ Groom with his entire family and/or any combination thereof

❑ Groom with his best man

❑ Groom with his ushers

❑ Groom shaking hands with his best man

❑ Groom with the bride's father

❑ Bride and her father getting out of the limousine

WEDDING PHOTOGRAPHS

Check off all photographs you would like taken throughout your wedding day.
Then make a copy of this form and give it to your photographer.

❑   Special members of the family being seated

❑   Groom waiting for the bride before the processional

❑   Bride and her father just before the processional

OTHER PRE-CEREMONY PHOTOS YOU WOULD LIKE

❑ _____

❑ _____

❑ _____

❑ _____

❑ _____

CEREMONY PHOTOGRAPHS

❑   The processional

❑   Bride and groom saying their vows

❑   Bride and groom exchanging rings

❑   Groom kissing the bride at the altar

❑   The recessional

OTHER CEREMONY PHOTOS YOU WOULD LIKE

❑ _____

❑ _____

❑ _____

❑ _____

❑ _____

WEDDING PHOTOGRAPHS

Check off all photographs you would like taken throughout your wedding day.
Then make a copy of this form and give it to your photographer.

POST-CEREMONY PHOTOGRAPHS

❑   Bride and groom

❑   Newlyweds with both of their families

❑   Newlyweds with the entire wedding party

❑   Bride and groom signing the marriage certificate

❑   Flowers and other decorations

OTHER POST-CEREMONY PHOTOS YOU WOULD LIKE

❑   _____

❑   _____

❑   _____

❑   _____

❑   _____

RECEPTION PHOTOGRAPHS

❑   Entrance of newlyweds and wedding party into the reception site

❑   Receiving line

❑   Guests signing the guest book

❑   Toasts

❑   First dance

❑   Bride and her father dancing

❑   Groom and his mother dancing

❑   Bride dancing with groom's father

❑   Groom dancing with bride's mother

❑   Wedding party and guests dancing

❑   Cake table

WEDDING PHOTOGRAPHS

Check off all photographs you would like taken throughout your wedding day.
Then make a copy of this form and give it to your photographer.

- ❑   Cake-cutting ceremony
- ❑   Couple feeding each other cake
- ❑   Table decorations
- ❑   Bouquet-tossing ceremony
- ❑   Garter-tossing ceremony
- ❑   Musicians
- ❑   The wedding party table
- ❑   The family tables
- ❑   Candid shots of your guests
- ❑   Bride and groom saying goodbye to their parents
- ❑   Bride and groom looking back, waving goodbye in the getaway car

OTHER RECEPTION PHOTOS YOU WOULD LIKE

- ❑   _____
- ❑   _____
- ❑   _____
- ❑   _____
- ❑   _____
- ❑   _____
- ❑   _____
- ❑   _____
- ❑   _____
- ❑   _____
- ❑   _____
- ❑   _____
- ❑   _____

VIDEOGRAPHER COMPARISON CHART

QUESTIONS	POSSIBILITY 1	POSSIBILITY 2
What is the name and phone number of the videographer?		
What is the website and e-mail address of the videographer?		
What is the address of the videographer?		
How many years of experience do you have as a videographer?		
Approximately how many weddings have you videotaped?		
Are you the person who will videotape my wedding?		
Will you bring an assistant with you to my wedding?		
What type of equipment do you use?		
Do you have a wireless microphone?		
Do you bring backup equipment with you?		
Do you visit the ceremony and reception sites before the wedding?		
Do you edit the tape after the event?		
Who keeps the raw footage and for how long?		
When will I receive the final product?		
What is the cost of the desired package?		
What does it include?		
Can you make a photo montage? What is the cost?		
Can you do a Same-Day Edit? What is the cost?		
What is your payment policy?		
What is your cancellation policy?		

QUESTIONS	POSSIBILITY 3	POSSIBILITY 4
What is the name and phone number of the videographer?		
What is the website and e-mail address of the videographer?		
What is the address of the videographer?		
How many years of experience do you have as a videographer?		
Approximately how many weddings have you videotaped?		
Are you the person who will videotape my wedding?		
Will you bring an assistant with you to my wedding?		
What type of equipment do you use?		
Do you have a wireless microphone?		
Do you bring backup equipment with you?		
Do you visit the ceremony and reception sites before the wedding?		
Do you edit the tape after the event?		
Who keeps the raw footage and for how long?		
When will I receive the final product?		
What is the cost of the desired package?		
What does it include?		
Can you make a photo montage? What is the cost?		
Can you do a Same-Day Edit? What is the cost?		
What is your payment policy?		
What is your cancellation policy?		

VIDEOGRAPHER'S INFORMATION

Once it is completed, make a copy of this form to give to your videographer as a reminder of your various events.

THE WEDDING OF: _____ Phone Number: _____

VIDEOGRAPHER'S COMPANY: _____

Business Name: _____

Address: _____

City: _____ State: _____ Zip Code: _____

Website: _____

E-mail: _____

Videographer's Name: _____ Phone Number: _____

Assistant's Name: _____ Phone Number: _____

CEREMONY: _____

Date: _____ Arrival Time: _____ Departure Time: _____

Location: _____

Address: _____

City: _____ State: _____ Zip Code: _____

Ceremony Restrictions/Guidelines: _____

RECEPTION: _____

Date: _____ Arrival Time: _____ Departure Time: _____

Location: _____

Address: _____

City: _____ State: _____ Zip Code: _____

Reception Restrictions/Guidelines: _____

STATIONERY
& GUEST LIST

KAREN FRENCH

KAREN FRENCH

KAREN FRENCH

KAREN FRENCH

KAREN FRENCH

KAREN FRENCH

KAREN FRENCH

STATIONERY CHECKLIST

ITEM	QUANTITY	COST
❏ Invitations		
❏ Envelopes		
❏ Response Cards/Envelopes		
❏ Reception Cards		
❏ Ceremony Cards		
❏ Pew Cards		
❏ Seating/Place Cards		
❏ Rain Cards		
❏ Maps		
❏ Ceremony Programs		
❏ Announcements		
❏ Thank-You Notes		
❏ Stamps		
❏ Personalized Napkins/Matchbooks		
❏ Other:		
❏ Other:		
❏ Other:		
❏ Other:		
❏ Other:		
❏ Other:		
❏ Other:		
❏ Other:		
❏ Other:		
❏ Other:		
❏ Other:		
❏ Other:		
❏ Other:		

ANNOUNCEMENT LIST

Make as many copies of this form as needed.

NAME: _____

Address: _____

City: _____

State: _____ Zip Code: _____

Phone Number: _____

Email: _____

NAME: _____

Address: _____

City: _____

State: _____ Zip Code: _____

Phone Number: _____

Email: _____

NAME: _____

Address: _____

City: _____

State: _____ Zip Code: _____

Phone Number: _____

Email: _____

NAME: _____

Address: _____

City: _____

State: _____ Zip Code: _____

Phone Number: _____

Email: _____

NAME: _____

Address: _____

City: _____

State: _____ Zip Code: _____

Phone Number: _____

Email: _____

NAME: _____

Address: _____

City: _____

State: _____ Zip Code: _____

Phone Number: _____

Email: _____

NAME: _____

Address: _____

City: _____

State: _____ Zip Code: _____

Phone Number: _____

Email: _____

NAME: _____

Address: _____

City: _____

State: _____ Zip Code: _____

Phone Number: _____

Email: _____

STATIONERY COMPARISON CHART

QUESTIONS	POSSIBILITY 1	POSSIBILITY 2
What is the name and phone number of the stationery provider?		
What is the website and e-mail of the stationery provider?		
What is the address of the stationery provider?		
How many years of experience do you have?		
What lines of stationery do you carry?		
What types of printing processes do you offer?		
How soon in advance does the order have to be placed?		
What is the turnaround time?		
What is the cost of the desired invitation? Announcement?		
What is the cost of the desired response card? Reception card?		
What is the cost of the desired thank-you note?		
What is the cost of the desired party favors?		
What is the cost of the desired wedding program?		
What is the cost of addressing the envelopes in calligraphy?		
What is your payment policy?		
What is your cancellation policy?		

QUESTIONS	POSSIBILITY 3	POSSIBILITY 4
What is the name and phone number of the stationery provider?		
What is the website and e-mail of the stationery provider?		
What is the address of the stationery provider?		
How many years of experience do you have?		
What lines of stationery do you carry?		
What types of printing processes do you offer?		
How soon in advance does the order have to be placed?		
What is the turnaround time?		
What is the cost of the desired invitation? Announcement?		
What is the cost of the desired response card? Reception card?		
What is the cost of the desired thank-you note?		
What is the cost of the desired party favors?		
What is the cost of the desired wedding program?		
What is the cost of addressing the envelopes in calligraphy?		
What is your payment policy?		
What is your cancellation policy?		

STATIONERY DESCRIPTION

STATIONER: _____ Date Ordered: _____

Salesperson: _____ Phone Number: _____

Address: _____

City: _____ State: _____ Zip Code: _____

Website: _____

E-mail: _____

STATIONERY ITEM: (Include selections for Paper, Style, Color, Font, Printing)

Invitations/Envelopes: _____

Response Cards/Envelopes: _____

Reception Cards: _____

Ceremony Cards: _____

Pew Cards: _____

Seating/Place Cards: _____

Rain Cards: _____

Maps: _____

Ceremony Programs: _____

Announcements: _____

Thank-You Notes: _____

Napkins: _____

Matchbooks: _____

❑ Other: _____

❑ Other: _____

❑ Other: _____

❑ Other: _____

❑ Other: _____

❑ Other: _____

STATIONERY WORDING

Invitations:
_____
_____
_____
_____
_____
_____
_____
_____
_____

Announcements:
_____
_____
_____

Reception Cards:
_____
_____
_____

Response Cards:
_____
_____
_____

Seating/Place Cards:
_____
_____
_____

Napkins/Matchbooks:
_____
_____
_____

MY GUEST LIST

NAME	# OF GUESTS	RSVP	GIFT RECEIVED	THANK-YOU SENT

NAME	# OF GUESTS	RSVP	GIFT RECEIVED	THANK-YOU SENT

NAME	# OF GUESTS	RSVP	GIFT RECEIVED	THANK-YOU SENT

NAME	# OF GUESTS	RSVP	GIFT RECEIVED	THANK-YOU SENT

NAME	# OF GUESTS	RSVP	GIFT RECEIVED	THANK-YOU SENT

NAME	# OF GUESTS	RSVP	GIFT RECEIVED	THANK-YOU SENT

THE BRIDE'S WEDDING PARTY

MAID OF HONOR: _____

Address: _____

Home Phone: _____ Cell Phone: _____

E-mail: _____ Wedding Party Gift: _____

BRIDESMAID: _____

Address: _____

Home Phone: _____ Cell Phone: _____

E-mail: _____ Wedding Party Gift: _____

BRIDESMAID: _____

Address: _____

Home Phone: _____ Cell Phone: _____

E-mail: _____ Wedding Party Gift: _____

BRIDESMAID: _____

Address: _____

Home Phone: _____ Cell Phone: _____

E-mail: _____ Wedding Party Gift: _____

BRIDESMAID: _____

Address: _____

Home Phone: _____ Cell Phone: _____

E-mail: _____ Wedding Party Gift: _____

BRIDESMAID: _____

Address: _____

Home Phone: _____ Cell Phone: _____

E-mail: _____ Wedding Party Gift: _____

THE GROOM'S WEDDING PARTY

BEST MAN: _____

Address: _____

Home Phone: _____ Cell Phone: _____

E-mail: _____ Wedding Party Gift: _____

GROOMSMAN: _____

Address: _____

Home Phone: _____ Cell Phone: _____

E-mail: _____ Wedding Party Gift: _____

GROOMSMAN: _____

Address: _____

Home Phone: _____ Cell Phone: _____

E-mail: _____ Wedding Party Gift: _____

GROOMSMAN: _____

Address: _____

Home Phone: _____ Cell Phone: _____

E-mail: _____ Wedding Party Gift: _____

GROOMSMAN: _____

Address: _____

Home Phone: _____ Cell Phone: _____

E-mail: _____ Wedding Party Gift: _____

GROOMSMAN: _____

Address: _____

Home Phone: _____ Cell Phone: _____

E-mail: _____ Wedding Party Gift: _____

GUIDELINES FOR ADDRESSING INVITATIONS

SITUATION	INNER ENVELOPE NO FIRST NAME OR ADDRESS	OUTER ENVELOPE HAS FIRST NAME & ADDRESS
Husband and Wife (with same surname)	Mr. and Mrs. Smith	Mr. and Mrs. Thomas Smith (use middle name, if known)
Husband and Wife (with different surnames)	Ms. Banks and Mr. Smith (wife first)	Ms. Anita Banks Mr. Thomas Smith (wife's name & title above husband's)
Husband and Wife (wife has professional title)	Dr. Smith and Mr. Smith	Dr. Anita Smith Mr. Thomas Smith (wife's name & title above husband's)
Husband and Wife (with children under 16)	Mr. and Mrs. Smith John, Mary, and Glen (in order of age)	Mr. and Mrs. Thomas Smith
Single Woman (regardless of age)	Miss/Ms. Smith	Miss/Ms. Beverly Smith
Single Woman and Guest	Miss/Ms. Smith Mr. Jones (or "and Guest")	Miss/Ms. Beverly Smith
Single Man	Mr. Jones (Master for a young boy)	Mr. William Jones
Single Man and Guest	Mr. Jones Miss/Ms. Smith (or "and Guest")	Mr. William Jones
Unmarried Couple Living Together	Mr. Knight and Ms. Orlandi (names listed alphabetically)	Mr. Michael Knight Ms. Paula Orlandi
Two Sisters (over 16)	The Misses Smith	The Misses Mary and Jane Smith (in order of age)
Two Brothers (over 16)	The Messrs. Smith	The Messrs. John and Glen Smith (in order of age)
Brothers & Sisters (over 16)	Mary, Jane, John & Glen (name the girls first, in order of age)	The Misses Smith The Messrs. Smith (name the girls first)
A Brother and Sister (over 16)	Jane and John (name the girl first)	Miss Jane Smith and Mr. John Smith (name the girl first)
Widow	Mrs. Smith	Mrs. William Smith
Divorcee	Mrs. Smith	Mrs. Jones Smith (maiden name and former husband's surname)

RECEPTION
& CATERING

5

KAREN FRENCH

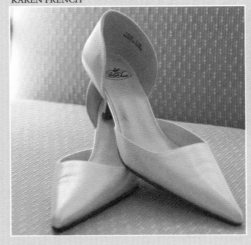

RECEPTION SITE COMPARISON CHART

QUESTIONS	POSSIBILITY 1	POSSIBILITY 2
What is the name of the reception site?		
What is the website and e-mail of the reception site?		
What is the address of the reception site?		
What is the name and phone number of my contact person?		
What dates and times are available?		
What is the maximum number of guests for a seated reception?		
What is the maximum number of guests for a cocktail reception?		
What is the reception site fee?		
What is the price range for a seated lunch?		
What is the price range for a buffet lunch?		
What is the price range for a seated dinner?		
What is the price range for a buffet dinner?		
What is the corkage fee?		
What is the cake-cutting fee?		
What is the ratio of servers to guests?		
How much time will be allotted for my reception?		
What music restrictions are there, if any?		
What alcohol restrictions are there, if any?		

QUESTIONS	POSSIBILITY 3	POSSIBILITY 4
What is the name of the reception site?		
What is the website and e-mail of the reception site?		
What is the address of the reception site?		
What is the name and phone number of my contact person?		
What dates and times are available?		
What is the maximum number of guests for a seated reception?		
What is the maximum number of guests for a cocktail reception?		
What is the reception site fee?		
What is the price range for a seated lunch?		
What is the price range for a buffet lunch?		
What is the price range for a seated dinner?		
What is the price range for a buffet dinner?		
What is the corkage fee?		
What is the cake-cutting fee?		
What is the ratio of servers to guests?		
How much time will be allotted for my reception?		
What music restrictions are there, if any?		
What alcohol restrictions are there, if any?		

QUESTIONS	POSSIBILITY 1	POSSIBILITY 2
Are there any restrictions for rice or rose petal tossing?		
What room and table decorations are available?		
Is a changing room available?		
Is there handicap accessibility?		
Is a dance floor included in the site fee?		
Are tables, chairs, and linens included in the site fee?		
Are outside caterers allowed?		
Are kitchen facilities available for outside caterers?		
Does the facility have full liability insurance?		
What perks or giveaways are offered?		
How many parking spaces are available for my wedding party?		
How many parking spaces are available for my guests?		
What is the cost for parking, if any?		
What is the cost for sleeping rooms, if available?		
What is the payment policy?		
What is the cancellation policy?		

QUESTIONS	POSSIBILITY 3	POSSIBILITY 4
Are there any restrictions for rice or rose petal tossing?		
What room and table decorations are available?		
Is a changing room available?		
Is there handicap accessibility?		
Is a dance floor included in the site fee?		
Are tables, chairs, and linens included in the site fee?		
Are outside caterers allowed?		
Are kitchen facilities available for outside caterers?		
Does the facility have full liability insurance?		
What perks or giveaways are offered?		
How many parking spaces are available for my wedding party?		
How many parking spaces are available for my guests?		
What is the cost for parking, if any?		
What is the cost for sleeping rooms, if available?		
What is the payment policy?		
What is the cancellation policy?		

RECEPTION SITE INFORMATION SHEET

RECEPTION SITE: _____

Site Coordinator: _____   Cost: _____

Website: _____

E-mail: _____

Phone Number: _____   Fax Number: _____

Address: _____

City: _____   State: _____   Zip Code: _____

Name of Room: _____   Room Capacity: _____

Date Confirmed: _____   Confirm Head Count By: __

Beginning Time: _____   Ending Time: _____

Cocktails/Hors d'Oeuvres Time: _____   Meal Time: _____

Color of Linens: _____   Color of Napkins: _____

Total Cost: _____

Deposit: _____   Date: _____

Balance: _____   Date Due: _____

Cancellation Policy: _____

EQUIPMENT INCLUDES:

❑ Tables   ❑ Chairs   ❑ Linens   ❑ Tableware   ❑ Barware

❑ Heaters   ❑ Electric Outlet   ❑ Musical Instruments

SERVICE INCLUDES:

❑ Waiters   ❑ Bartenders   ❑ Valet   ❑ Main Meal

❑ Clean Up   ❑ Setup   ❑ Security   ❑ Free Parking

CATERER INFORMATION SHEET

CATERER: _____

Contact Person: _____ Cost Per Person: _____

Website: _____

E-mail: _____

Phone Number: _____ Fax Number: _____

Address: _____

City: _____ State: _____ Zip Code: _____

Confirmed Date: _____ Confirm Head Count By: _____

Arrival Time: _____ Departure Time: _____

Cocktails/Hors d'Oeuvres Time: _____ Meal Time: _____

Color of Linens: _____ Color of Napkins: _____

Total Cost: _____

Deposit: _____ Date: _____

Balance: _____ Date Due: _____

Cancellation Policy: _____

EQUIPMENT INCLUDES:

❑ Tables ❑ Chairs ❑ Linens ❑ Tableware

❑ Barware ❑ Heaters ❑ Lighting ❑ Candles

SERVICE INCLUDES:

❑ Waiters ❑ Bartenders ❑ Setup ❑ Clean Up

❑ Security ❑ Hors d'Oeuvres ❑ Buffet Meal ❑ Seated Meal

❑ Cocktails ❑ Champagne ❑ Wine ❑ Beer

❑ Punch ❑ Soft Drinks ❑ Coffee/Tea ❑ Cake

TABLE SEATING ARRANGEMENTS

Complete this form only after finalizing your guest list. Make as many copies of this form as needed.

HEAD TABLE	BRIDE'S FAMILY TABLE	GROOM'S FAMILY TABLE
_____	_____	_____
_____	_____	_____
_____	_____	_____
_____	_____	_____
_____	_____	_____
_____	_____	_____
_____	_____	_____
_____	_____	_____

• TABLE _____   • TABLE _____   • TABLE _____

_____	_____	_____
_____	_____	_____
_____	_____	_____
_____	_____	_____
_____	_____	_____
_____	_____	_____
_____	_____	_____
_____	_____	_____

• TABLE _____   • TABLE _____   • TABLE _____

_____	_____	_____
_____	_____	_____
_____	_____	_____
_____	_____	_____
_____	_____	_____

TABLE SEATING ARRANGEMENTS

Complete this form only after finalizing your guest list. Make as many copies of this form as needed.

• TABLE _____

_____
_____
_____
_____
_____
_____
_____
_____

• TABLE _____

_____
_____
_____
_____
_____
_____
_____
_____

• TABLE _____

_____
_____
_____
_____
_____
_____
_____
_____

• TABLE _____

_____
_____
_____
_____
_____
_____
_____
_____

• TABLE _____

_____
_____
_____
_____
_____
_____
_____
_____

• TABLE _____

_____
_____
_____
_____
_____
_____
_____
_____

• TABLE _____

_____
_____
_____
_____
_____
_____

• TABLE _____

_____
_____
_____
_____
_____
_____

• TABLE _____

_____
_____
_____
_____
_____
_____

CATERER COMPARISON CHART

QUESTIONS	POSSIBILITY 1	POSSIBILITY 2
What is the name of the caterer?		
What is the website and e-mail of the caterer?		
What is the address of the caterer?		
What is the name and phone number of my contact person?		
How many years have you been in business?		
What percentage of your business is dedicated to receptions?		
Do you have liability insurance/license to serve alcohol?		
When is the final head-count needed?		
What is your ratio of servers to guests?		
How do your servers dress for wedding receptions?		
What is your price range for a seated lunch/buffet lunch?		
What is your price range for a seated/buffet dinner?		
How much gratuity is expected?		
What is your specialty?		
What is your cake-cutting fee?		
What is your bartending fee?		
What is your fee to clean up after the reception?		
What is your payment policy?		
What is your cancellation policy?		

QUESTIONS	POSSIBILITY 3	POSSIBILITY 4
What is the name of the caterer?		
What is the website and e-mail of the caterer?		
What is the address of the caterer?		
What is the name and phone number of my contact person?		
How many years have you been in business?		
What percentage of your business is dedicated to receptions?		
Do you have liability insurance/license to serve alcohol?		
When is the final head-count needed?		
What is your ratio of servers to guests?		
How do your servers dress for wedding receptions?		
What is your price range for a seated lunch/buffet lunch?		
What is your price range for a seated/buffet dinner?		
How much gratuity is expected?		
What is your specialty?		
What is your cake-cutting fee?		
What is your bartending fee?		
What is your fee to clean up after the reception?		
What is your payment policy?		
What is your cancellation policy?		

PARTY FAVORS COMPARISON CHART

Party favors might include matchbooks, personalized wine bottles, chocolates, candies, or frames.

TYPE OF FAVOR	WEBSITE/COMPANY	QUANTITY	PRICE

LIQUOR ORDER FORM

LIQUOR VENDOR: _____   Date Ordered: _____

Salesperson: _____   Phone Number: _____

Website: _____

E-mail: _____

Address: _____

City: _____ State: _____ Zip Code: _____

Cost: _____

Delivered By: _____   Delivery Date: _____

TYPE OF LIQUOR	# OF BOTTLES NEEDED	PRICE

MENU WORKSHEET

HORS D'OEUVRES: _____
_____
_____
_____

SALADS/APPETIZERS: _____
_____
_____
_____

SOUPS: _____
_____
_____
_____

MAIN ENTREE: _____
_____
_____
_____

DESSERTS: _____
_____
_____
_____

WEDDING CAKE: _____
_____
_____
_____

GUEST ACCOMMODATION LIST

Make as many copies of this form as needed to accommodate the size of your guest list.

NAME: _____   NAME: _____

Arrival Date: _____ Time: _____   Arrival Date: _____ Time: _____

Airline/Flight #: _____   Airline/Flight #: _____

Accommodation: _____   Accommodation: _____

Departure Date: _____ Time: _____   Departure Date: _____ Time: _____

Airline/Flight #: _____   Airline/Flight #: _____

Phone: _____   Phone: _____

NAME: _____   NAME: _____

Arrival Date: _____ Time: _____   Arrival Date: _____ Time: _____

Airline/Flight #: _____   Airline/Flight #: _____

Accommodation: _____   Accommodation: _____

Departure Date: _____ Time: _____   Departure Date: _____ Time: _____

Airline/Flight #: _____   Airline/Flight #: _____

Phone: _____   Phone: _____

NAME: _____   NAME: _____

Arrival Date: _____ Time: _____   Arrival Date: _____ Time: _____

Airline/Flight #: _____   Airline/Flight #: _____

Accommodation: _____   Accommodation: _____

Departure Date: _____ Time: _____   Departure Date: _____ Time: _____

Airline/Flight #: _____   Airline/Flight #: _____

Phone: _____   Phone: _____

MUSIC &
BAKERY

KAREN FRENCH

CEREMONY MUSIC COMPARISON CHART

QUESTIONS	POSSIBILITY 1	POSSIBILITY 2
What is the name of the musician or band?		
What is the website and e-mail of the musician or band?		
What is the address of the musician or band?		
What is the name and phone number of my contact person?		
How many years of professional experience do you have?		
What percentage of your business is dedicated to weddings?		
Are you the person who will perform at my wedding?		
What instrument(s) do you play?		
What type of music do you specialize in?		
What are your hourly fees?		
What is the cost of a soloist?		
What is the cost of a duet?		
What is the cost of a trio?		
What is the cost of a quartet?		
How would you dress for my wedding?		
Do you have liability insurance?		
Do you have a cordless microphone?		
What is your payment/cancellation policy?		

QUESTIONS	POSSIBILITY 3	POSSIBILITY 4
What is the name of the musician or band?		
What is the website and e-mail of the musician or band?		
What is the address of the musician or band?		
What is the name and phone number of my contact person?		
How many years of professional experience do you have?		
What percentage of your business is dedicated to weddings?		
Are you the person who will perform at my wedding?		
What instrument(s) do you play?		
What type of music do you specialize in?		
What are your hourly fees?		
What is the cost of a soloist?		
What is the cost of a duet?		
What is the cost of a trio?		
What is the cost of a quartet?		
How would you dress for my wedding?		
Do you have liability insurance?		
Do you have a cordless microphone?		
What is your payment/cancellation policy?		

RECEPTION MUSIC COMPARISON CHART

QUESTIONS	POSSIBILITY 1	POSSIBILITY 2
What is the name of the musician? Band? DJ?		
What is the website and e-mail of the musician? Band? DJ?		
What is the address of the musician? Band? DJ?		
What is the name and phone number of my contact person?		
How many years of professional experience do you have?		
What percentage of your business is dedicated to receptions?		
How many people are in your band?		
What type of music do you specialize in?		
What type of sound system do you have?		
Can you act as a master of ceremonies? How do you dress?		
Can you provide a light show?		
Do you have a cordless microphone?		
How many breaks do you take? How long are they?		
Do you play recorded music during breaks?		
Do you have liability insurance?		
What are your fees for a 4-hour reception?		
What is your cost for each additional hour?		

QUESTIONS	POSSIBILITY 3	POSSIBILITY 4
What is the name of the musician? Band? DJ?		
What is the website and e-mail of the musician? Band? DJ?		
What is the address of the musician? Band? DJ?		
What is the name and phone number of my contact person?		
How many years of professional experience do you have?		
What percentage of your business is dedicated to receptions?		
How many people are in your band?		
What type of music do you specialize in?		
What type of sound system do you have?		
Can you act as a master of ceremonies? How do you dress?		
Can you provide a light show?		
Do you have a cordless microphone?		
How many breaks do you take? How long are they?		
Do you play recorded music during breaks?		
Do you have liability insurance?		
What are your fees for a 4-hour reception?		
What is your cost for each additional hour?		

CEREMONY MUSIC SELECTIONS

Make a copy of this form and give it to your musicians.

WHEN	SELECTION	COMPOSER	PLAYED BY
Prelude 1			
Prelude 2			
Prelude 3			
Processional			
Bride's Processional			
Ceremony 1			
Ceremony 2			
Ceremony 3			
Recessional			
Postlude			
Other:			
Other:			
Other:			
Other:			
Other:			
Other:			

RECEPTION MUSIC SELECTIONS

Make a copy of this form and give it to your musicians.

WHEN	SELECTION	SONGWRITER	PLAYED BY
Receiving Line			
During Hors d'Oeuvres			
During Dinner			
First Dance			
Second Dance			
Third Dance			
Bouquet Toss			
Garter Removal			
Cutting of the Cake			
Last Dance			
Couple Leaving			
Other:			
Other:			
Other:			
Other:			
Other:			
Other:			

BAKERY COMPARISON CHART

QUESTIONS	POSSIBILITY 1	POSSIBILITY 2
What is the name of the bakery?		
What is the bakery's website and e-mail?		
What is the address of the bakery?		
What is the name and phone number of my contact person?		
How many years have you been making wedding cakes?		
What are your wedding cake specialties?		
Do you offer free tasting of your wedding cakes?		
Are your wedding cakes fresh or frozen?		
How far in advance should I order my cake?		
Can you make a groom's cake?		
Do you lend, rent, or sell cake knives?		
What is the cost per serving of my desired cake?		
What is your cake pillar and plate rental fee, if any?		
Is this fee refundable upon the return of these items?		
When must these items be returned?		
What is your cake delivery and setup fee?		
What is your payment policy?		
What is your cancellation policy?		

BAKERY COMPARISON CHART (CONT.)

QUESTIONS	POSSIBILITY 3	POSSIBILITY 4
What is the name of the bakery?		
What is the bakery's website and e-mail?		
What is the address of the bakery?		
What is the name and phone number of my contact person?		
How many years have you been making wedding cakes?		
What are your wedding cake specialties?		
Do you offer free tasting of your wedding cakes?		
Are your wedding cakes fresh or frozen?		
How far in advance should I order my cake?		
Can you make a groom's cake?		
Do you lend, rent, or sell cake knives?		
What is the cost per serving of my desired cake?		
What is your cake pillar and plate rental fee, if any?		
Is this fee refundable upon the return of these items?		
When must these items be returned?		
What is your cake delivery and setup fee?		
What is your payment policy?		
What is your cancellation policy?		

CAKE TASTING CHART

BAKERY OPTION 1

Company Name: _____ Contact Person: _____

FLAVOR	PRICE PER SLICE	NOTES
1)	$	
2)	$	
3)	$	

BAKERY OPTION 2

Company Name: _____ Contact Person: _____

FLAVOR	PRICE PER SLICE	NOTES
1)	$	
2)	$	
3)	$	

BAKERY OPTION 3

Company Name: _____ Contact Person: _____

FLAVOR	PRICE PER SLICE	NOTES
1)	$	
2)	$	
3)	$	

NOTES

FLOWERS & DECORATIONS

KAREN FRENCH

FLORIST COMPARISON CHART

QUESTIONS	POSSIBILITY 1	POSSIBILITY 2
What is the name of the florist?		
What is the website and e-mail of the florist?		
What is the address of the florist?		
What are your business hours?		
What is the name and phone number of my contact person?		
How many years of professional floral experience do you have?		
What percentage of your business is dedicated to weddings?		
Do you have access to out-of-season flowers?		
Will you visit my wedding sites to make floral recommendations?		
Can you preserve my bridal bouquet?		
Do you rent vases and candle holders?		
Can you provide silk flowers?		
What is the cost of the desired bridal bouquet?		
What is the cost of the desired boutonniere?		
What is the cost of the desired corsage?		
Do you have liability insurance?		
What are your delivery/setup fees?		
What is your payment/cancellation policy?		

QUESTIONS	POSSIBILITY 3	POSSIBILITY 4
What is the name of the florist?		
What is the website and e-mail of the florist?		
What is the address of the florist?		
What are your business hours?		
What is the name and phone number of my contact person?		
How many years of professional floral experience do you have?		
What percentage of your business is dedicated to weddings?		
Do you have access to out-of-season flowers?		
Will you visit my wedding sites to make floral recommendations?		
Can you preserve my bridal bouquet?		
Do you rent vases and candle holders?		
Can you provide silk flowers?		
What is the cost of the desired bridal bouquet?		
What is the cost of the desired boutonniere?		
What is the cost of the desired corsage?		
Do you have liability insurance?		
What are your delivery/setup fees?		
What is your payment/cancellation policy?		

FLOWERS AND THEIR SEASONS

FLOWER	WINTER	SPRING	SUMMER	FALL
Allium		X	X	
Alstroemeria	X	X	X	X
Amaryllis	X		X	
Anemone	X	X		X
Aster	X	X	X	X
Baby's Breath	X	X	X	X
Bachelor's Button	X	X	X	X
Billy Buttons		X	X	
Bird of Paradise	X	X	X	X
Bouvardia	X	X	X	X
Calla Lily	X	X	X	X
Carnation	X	X	X	X
Celosia		X	X	
Chrysanthemum	X	X	X	X
Daffodils		X		
Dahlia			X	X
Delphinium			X	X
Eucalyptus	X	X	X	X
Freesia	X	X	X	X
Gardenia	X	X	X	X
Gerbera	X	X	X	X
Gladiolus	X	X	X	X
Iris	X	X	X	X
Liatris	X	X	X	X
Lily	X	X	X	X

FLOWERS AND THEIR SEASONS

FLOWER	WINTER	SPRING	SUMMER	FALL
Lily of the Valley		X		
Lisianthus		X	X	X
Narcissus	X	X		X
Nerine	X	X	X	X
Orchid (Cattleya)	X	X	X	X
Orchid (Cymbidium)	X	X	X	X
Peony		X		
Pincushion			X	
Protea	X			X
Queen Anne's Lace			X	
Ranunculas		X		
Rose	X	X	X	X
Saponaria			X	
Snapdragon		X	X	X
Speedwell			X	
Star of Bethlehem	X			X
Statice	X	X	X	X
Stephanotis	X	X	X	X
Stock	X	X	X	X
Sunflower		X	X	X
Sweet Pea		X		
Tuberose			X	X
Tulip	X	X		
Waxflower	X	X		

BOUQUETS AND FLOWERS

BRIDE'S BOUQUET

Color Scheme: _____

Style: _____

Flowers: _____

_____

_____

Greenery: _____

Other (Ribbons, etc.): _____

MAID OF HONOR'S BOUQUET

Color Scheme: _____

Style: _____

Flowers: _____

_____

_____

Greenery: _____

Other (Ribbons, etc.): _____

BRIDESMAIDS' BOUQUETS

Color Scheme: _____

Style: _____

Flowers: _____

_____

_____

Greenery: _____

Other (Ribbons, etc.): _____

BOUQUETS AND FLOWERS

FLOWER GIRL'S BOUQUET

Color Scheme: _____

Style: _____

Flowers: _____

_____

_____

Greenery: _____

Other (Ribbons, etc.): _____

_____

OTHER

Groom's Boutonniere: _____

_____

_____

Ushers' and Other Family Members' Boutonnieres: _____

_____

_____

Mother of the Bride Corsage: _____

_____

_____

Mother of the Groom Corsage: _____

_____

_____

Altar or Chuppah: _____

_____

_____

Steps to Altar or Chuppah: _____

_____

BOUQUETS AND FLOWERS

OTHER

Pews: _____
_____
_____

Entrance to the Ceremony: _____
_____
_____

Entrance to the Reception: _____
_____
_____

Receiving Line: _____
_____
_____

Head Table: _____
_____
_____

Parents' Table: _____
_____
_____

Guest Table: _____
_____
_____

Cake Table: _____
_____

Serving Table (Buffet, Dessert): _____
_____

Gift Table: _____
_____

DECORATIONS CHART

TYPE OF DECORATION	DESCRIPTION	WEBSITE/COMPANY	QUANTITY	PRICE
Themed Decorations				
Guest Book				
Seating Cards				
Table Numbers				
Head Table Centerpiece				
Guest Tables' Centerpieces				
Other:				
Other:				
Other:				

TRANSPORTATION & RENTALS

KAREN FRENCH

TRANSPORTATION & RENTALS

TRANSPORTATION COMPARISON CHART

QUESTIONS	POSSIBILITY 1	POSSIBILITY 2
What is the name of the transportation service?		
What is the website and e-mail of the transportation service?		
What is the address of the transportation service?		
What is the name and phone number of my contact person?		
How many years have you been in business?		
How many vehicles do you have available?		
Can you provide a back-up vehicle in case of an emergency?		
What types of vehicles are available?		
What are the various sizes of vehicles available?		
How old are the vehicles?		
How many drivers are available?		
Can you show me photos of your drivers?		
How do your drivers dress for weddings?		
Do you have liability insurance?		
What is the minimum amount of time required to rent a vehicle?		
What is the cost per hour? Two hours? Three hours?		
How much gratuity is expected?		
What is your payment/cancellation policy?		

QUESTIONS	POSSIBILITY 3	POSSIBILITY 4
What is the name of the transportation service?		
What is the website and e-mail of the transportation service?		
What is the address of the transportation service?		
What is the name and phone number of my contact person?		
How many years have you been in business?		
How many vehicles do you have available?		
Can you provide a back-up vehicle in case of an emergency?		
What types of vehicles are available?		
What are the various sizes of vehicles available?		
How old are the vehicles?		
How many drivers are available?		
Can you show me photos of your drivers?		
How do your drivers dress for weddings?		
Do you have liability insurance?		
What is the minimum amount of time required to rent a vehicle?		
What is the cost per hour? Two hours? Three hours?		
How much gratuity is expected?		
What is your payment/cancellation policy?		

WEDDING DAY TRANSPORTATION CHART

TO CEREMONY SITE

NAME	PICKUP TIME	PICKUP LOCATION	VEHICLE/DRIVER
Bride			
Groom			
Bride's Parents			
Groom's Parents			
Bridesmaids			
Ushers			
Other:			
Other:			
Other:			

TO RECEPTION SITE

NAME	PICKUP TIME	PICKUP LOCATION	VEHICLE/DRIVER
Bride and Groom			
Bride's Parents			
Groom's Parents			
Bridesmaids			
Ushers			
Other:			
Other:			

CEREMONY EQUIPMENT CHECKLIST

RENTAL SUPPLIER: _____ Contact Person: _____

Website: _____

E-mail: _____

Address: _____

City: _____ State: _____ Zip Code: _____

Phone Number: _____ Hours: _____

Payment Policy: _____

Cancellation Policy: _____

Delivery Time: _____ Tear-Down Time: _____

Setup Time: _____ Pickup Time: _____

QTY.	ITEM	DESCRIPTION	PRICE	TOTAL
	Arch/Altar		$	$
	Canopy (Chuppah)		$	$
	Backdrops		$	$
	Floor Candelabra		$	$
	Candles		$	$
	Candle lighters		$	$
	Kneeling Bench		$	$
	Aisle Stanchions		$	$
	Aisle Runners		$	$
	Guest Book Stand		$	$
	Gift Table		$	$
	Chairs		$	$
	Audio Equipment		$	$
	Lighting		$	$
	Heating/Cooling		$	$
	Umbrellas/Tents		$	$
	Bug Eliminator		$	$
	Coat/Hat Rack		$	$
	Garbage Cans		$	$

QUESTIONS	POSSIBILITY 1	POSSIBILITY 2
What is the name of the party rental supplier?		
What is the address of the party rental supplier?		
What is the web site and e-mail of the party rental supplier?		
What is the name and phone number of my contact person?		
How many years have you been in business?		
What are your hours of operation?		
Do you have liability insurance?		
What is the cost per item needed?		
What is the cost of pickup and delivery?		
What is the cost of setting up the items rented?		
When would the items be delivered?		
When would the items be picked up after the event?		
What is your payment policy?		
What is your cancellation policy?		

QUESTIONS	POSSIBILITY 3	POSSIBILITY 4
What is the name of the party rental supplier?		
What is the address of the party rental supplier?		
What is the web site and e-mail of the party rental supplier?		
What is the name and phone number of my contact person?		
How many years have you been in business?		
What are your hours of operation?		
Do you have liability insurance?		
What is the cost per item needed?		
What is the cost of pickup and delivery?		
What is the cost of setting up the items rented?		
When would the items be delivered?		
When would the items be picked up after the event?		
What is your payment policy?		
What is your cancellation policy?		

RECEPTION EQUIPMENT CHECKLIST

RENTAL SUPPLIER: _____ Contact Person: _____

Website: _____

E-mail: _____

Address: _____

City: _____ State: _____ Zip Code: _____

Phone Number: _____ Hours: _____

Payment Policy: _____

Cancellation Policy: _____

Delivery Time: _____ Tear-Down Time: _____

Setup Time: _____ Pickup Time: _____

QTY.	ITEM	DESCRIPTION	PRICE	TOTAL
	Audio Equipment		$	$
	Cake Table		$	$
	Candelabras/Candles		$	$
	Canopies		$	$
	Coat/Hat Rack		$	$
	Dance Floor		$	$
	Bug Eliminator		$	$
	Garbage Cans		$	$
	Gift Table		$	$
	Guest Tables		$	$
	Heating/Cooling		$	$
	High/Booster Chairs		$	$
	Lighting		$	$
	Mirror Disco Ball		$	$
	Place Card Table		$	$
	Tents		$	$
	Umbrellas		$	$
	Visual Equipment		$	$
	Wheelchair Ramp		$	$

HONEYMOON

© ISTOCK PHOTO/
MICHAEL SVOBODA

HONEYMOON WISHLIST

LOCATION	BRIDE	GROOM
Hot Weather		
Mild Weather		
Cold Weather		
Dry Climate		
Moist Climate		
Beaches		
Lakes		
Forests		
Mountains		
Fields		
Sunsets		
Small Town		
Big City		
Popular Tourist Destination		
Visiting Among the Locals		
Nighttime Weather Conducive to Outdoor Activities		
Nighttime Weather Conducive to Indoor Activities		
"Modern" Resources and Services Available		
"Roughing It" On Your Own		
Culture and Customs You Are Familiar and Comfortable With		
New Cultures and Customs You Would Like to Get to Know		

ACCOMMODATIONS	BRIDE	GROOM
All-Inclusive Resort Community		
Lodging with Families		
Lodging with Adults Only		

HONEYMOON WISHLIST

ACCOMMODATIONS	BRIDE	GROOM
Lodging with Couples Only		
Lodging with Newlyweds Only		
Multi-Room Suite		
Champagne or Newlyweds Gifts in Room		
Minibar		
Flatscreen TV		
Fireplace in Room		
Balcony		
Private Jacuzzi in Room		
In-Room Massages		
Laundry Room on Premises		
Laundry/Dry Cleaning Service Available		
Bar/Lounge on Premises		
Spa on Premises		
Salon on Premises		
Gym on Premises		
Pool on Premises		
Poolside Bar		
Sauna or Hot Tub on Premises		
Fine Dining on Premises		

MEALS	BRIDE	GROOM
Casual Dining		
Formal Dining		
Fine Dining on Hotel Premises		
Prepared Yourself/Grocery Store		

HONEYMOON WISHLIST

MEALS	BRIDE	GROOM
Variety of Local and Regional Cuisine		
Traditional American Cuisine		
Opportunity for Picnics		
Exotic, International Menu		
Entertainment While Dining		
Set Meal Times		
Dining Based on Your Own Schedule		
Fast Food Restaurants		
Vegetarian/Special Diet Meals		
Delis, Diners		

ACTIVITIES	BRIDE	GROOM
Sunbathing		
Snorkeling		
Diving		
Swimming		
Jet Skiing		
Water Skiing		
Fishing		
Sailing		
Skiing/ Snowboarding		
Hiking		
Rock Climbing		
Camping		
Golf		
Tennis		

HONEYMOON WISHLIST

ACTIVITIES	BRIDE	GROOM
Bike Riding		
Boating		
Bus/Guided Tours		
Walking Tours		
Historic Sites/Tours		
Sightseeing on Your Own		
Art Museums		
Theatre		

NIGHTLIFE	BRIDE	GROOM
Dancing		
Theatre/Shows		
Gambling/Casinos		
Bars/Pubs		
Nightclubs		
Wine Tasting		
Live Music		
Art Exhibitions		
Quiet Strolls		
Stargazing		
Relaxing in Front of a Fireplace		
Being Out with the Locals		
Being Out with Other Newlyweds		

HONEYMOON BUDGET

Amount from the wedding budget set aside for the honeymoon	$
Amount groom is able to contribute from current funds/savings	$
Amount bride is able to contribute from current funds/savings	$
Amount to be saved/acquired by groom from now until the honeymoon date (monthly contributions, part-time job, gifts, bonuses)	$
Amount to be saved/acquired by bride from now until the honeymoon date (monthly contributions, part-time job, gifts, bonuses)	$
Amount from honeymoon registry and/or the Dollar Dance	$
Other contributions (family, etc.)	$

BUDGET TOTAL AMOUNT:	$

HONEYMOON PACKING LIST

TRAVELERS' FIRST AID KIT

- ❏ Aspirin
- ❏ Antacid tablets
- ❏ Diarrhea medication
- ❏ Cold remedies/sinus decongestant
- ❏ Throat lozenges
- ❏ Antiseptic lotion
- ❏ Band-Aids
- ❏ Blister-prevention stick
- ❏ Breath mints
- ❏ Chapstick
- ❏ Insect repellent, insect bite medication
- ❏ Sunblock and sunburn relief lotion
- ❏ Lotion/hand cream
- ❏ Eye drops or eye lubricant
- ❏ Hand sanitizer

- ❏ Vitamins
- ❏ Birth control
- ❏ Physicians' names, addresses, and telephone numbers
- ❏ Names and phone numbers of people to contact in case of an emergency
- ❏ Health insurance phone numbers
  Note: Be sure to contact your provider to find out about coverage while traveling in the U.S. and abroad.
- ❏ Prescription drugs
  Note: These should be kept in their original pharmacy containers that provide both drug and doctor information. Be sure to note the drug's generic name. You will want to pack these in your carry-on baggage in case the bags you've checked become lost or delayed.
- ❏ Medicine prescriptions (including generic names) and eyeglass prescription information (or an extra pair), list of food and drug allergies

PACKING CHECKLIST

CARRY-ON BAGGAGE

- ❏ Travelers' First Aid Kit
- ❏ Wallet (credit cards, traveler's checks)
- ❏ Jewelry and other sentimental and valuable items that you must bring
- ❏ Identification (passport, driver's license)

Photocopies of the following important documents:

- ❏ Airline tickets
- ❏ Hotel/resort street address, phone number, written confirmation of arrangements and reservations

- ❏ Complete travel itinerary
- ❏ Name, address and phone number of emergency contact person(s) back home
- ❏ Medicine prescriptions (including generic names) and eyeglass prescription information (or an extra pair), list of food and drug allergies
- ❏ Phone numbers (including after-hour emergency phone numbers) for health insurance company and personal physicians
- ❏ Phone numbers to the local U.S. embassy or consulate

HONEYMOON PACKING LIST

❏ List of your traveler's checks' serial numbers and 24-hour phone number for reporting loss or theft

❏ Copy of your packing list. This will help you while packing up at the end of your trip. It will also be invaluable if a piece of your luggage gets lost, as you will know the contents that are missing.

❏ Warm sweater or jacket

❏ Any "essential" toiletries and makeup and one complete casual outfit in case checked baggage is delayed or lost

❏ Foreign language dictionary or translator

❏ Camera

❏ Maps and guide books

❏ Small bills/change (in U.S. dollars and in the appropriate foreign currency) for tipping

❏ Currency converter chart or calculator

❏ Reading material

❏ Music player or portable DVD player

❏ Eyeglasses

❏ Contact lenses

❏ Contact lens cleaner

❏ Sunglasses

❏ Kleenex, gum, breath mints, and any over-the-counter medicine to ease travel discomfort

❏ Neck pillow and blanket

❏ Address book and thank-you notes (in case you have lots of traveling time)

❏ This book

❏ Your budget sheet

CHECKED BAGGAGE

CLOTHING

Casual Wear: *Consider the total number of each casual outfit item that you will need.*

❏ Shorts

❏ Pants

❏ Tops

❏ Jackets/sweaters

❏ Sweatshirts/sweatsuits

❏ Belts

❏ Socks

❏ Underwear/panties & bras

❏ Walking shoes/sandals/flip-flops

Athletic Wear: *Consider the total number of each sporting outfit item that you will need.*

❏ Shorts

❏ Sweatpants

❏ Tops

❏ Sweatshirts/jackets

❏ Swimsuits, swimsuit cover-up

❏ Aerobic activity outfit

❏ Athletic equipment

❏ Socks

❏ Underwear/panties & exercise bras

❏ Running/hiking shoes

HONEYMOON PACKING LIST

Evening Wear: *Consider the total number of each evening outfit item that you will need.*

- ❏ Pants/skirts/dresses
- ❏ Belts
- ❏ Dress shirts/blouses
- ❏ Sweaters
- ❏ Jackets/blazers/ties
- ❏ Socks or panty hose/slips
- ❏ Underwear/panties & bras
- ❏ Accessories/jewelry
- ❏ Shoes/heels
- ❏ Pajamas
- ❏ Lingerie
- ❏ Slippers
- ❏ Robe

Formal Wear: *Consider the number of each formal outfit item that you will need.*

- ❏ Dress pants/suits/tuxedo
- ❏ Dresses/gowns
- ❏ Accessories/jewelry
- ❏ Socks or panty hose/slips
- ❏ Underwear/panties & bras
- ❏ Dress shoes/heels

MISCELLANEOUS ITEMS

- ❏ An additional set of the important document photocopies as packed in your carry-on bag
- ❏ Travel tour books, tourism bureau information numbers
- ❏ Journal
- ❏ Special honeymoon gift for your new spouse
- ❏ Any romantic items or favorite accessories
- ❏ Camera and phone chargers

- ❏ Plastic bags for dirty laundry
- ❏ Large plastic or nylon tote bag for bringing home new purchases
- ❏ Small sewing kit and safety pins
- ❏ Hair-styling tools
- ❏ Travel iron, lint brush
- ❏ Compact umbrella, fold-up rain slickers
- ❏ Travel alarm clock
- ❏ Video camera

HONEYMOON PACKING LIST

FOR INTERNATIONAL TRAVEL

- ☐ Passports/visas
- ☐ Electric converters and adapter plugs
- ☐ Copy of appropriate forms showing proof of required vaccinations/ inoculations

Other items:

- ☐ _____
- ☐ _____
- ☐ _____
- ☐ _____
- ☐ _____
- ☐ _____
- ☐ _____

ITEMS TO LEAVE BEHIND
(with a trusted contact person)

- ☐ Photocopy of all travel details (complete itineraries, names, addresses, and telephone numbers)
- ☐ Photocopy of credit cards along with 24-hour telephone number to report loss or theft. (Be sure to get the number to call when traveling abroad. It will be a different number than their U.S. 1-800 number.)
- ☐ Photocopy of traveler's checks with 24-hour phone number to report loss or theft
- ☐ Photocopy of passport identification page, along with date and place of issuance
- ☐ Photocopy of driver's license
- ☐ Any irreplaceable items

Other items:

- ☐ _____
- ☐ _____
- ☐ _____
- ☐ _____
- ☐ _____
- ☐ _____
- ☐ _____
- ☐ _____
- ☐ _____
- ☐ _____
- ☐ _____
- ☐ _____

TIMELINES
& CALENDAR

KAREN FRENCH

KAREN FRENCH

KAREN FRENCH

KAREN FRENCH

KAREN FRENCH

KAREN FRENCH

This is a sample timeline.
Create your own timeline on the following pages.

TIME	DESCRIPTION	BRIDE	BRIDE'S MOTHER	BRIDE'S FATHER	MAID OF HONOR	BRIDESMAIDS	BRIDE'S FAMILY	GROOM	GROOM'S MOTHER	GROOM'S FATHER	BEST MAN	USHERS	GROOM'S FAMILY	FLOWER GIRL	RING BEARER
2:00 PM	MANICURIST APPOINTMENT	✓	✓		✓	✓									
2:30 PM	HAIR/MAKEUP APPOINTMENT	✓	✓		✓	✓									
4:15 PM	ARRIVE AT DRESSING SITE	✓	✓		✓	✓									
4:30 PM	ARRIVE AT DRESSING SITE							✓			✓	✓			
4:45 PM	PRE-CEREMONY PHOTOS							✓	✓	✓	✓	✓	✓		
5:15 PM	ARRIVE AT CEREMONY SITE							✓	✓	✓	✓	✓	✓		
5:15 PM	PRE-CEREMONY PHOTOS	✓	✓	✓	✓	✓	✓								
5:20 PM	GIVE OFFICIANT MARRIAGE LICENSE AND FEES										✓				
5:20 PM	USHERS RECEIVE SEATING CHART											✓			
5:30 PM	USHERS DISTRIBUTE WEDDING PROGRAMS AS GUESTS ARRIVE											✓			
5:30 PM	ARRIVE AT CEREMONY SITE													✓	✓
5:30 PM	GUEST BOOK ATTENDANT DIRECTS GUESTS TO SIGN BOOK														
5:30 PM	PRELUDE MUSIC BEGINS														
5:35 PM	USHERS BEGIN SEATING GUESTS											✓			
5:45 PM	ARRIVE AT CEREMONY SITE	✓	✓	✓	✓	✓	✓								
5:45 PM	USHERS SEAT HONORED GUESTS											✓			
5:50 PM	USHERS SEAT GROOM'S PARENTS								✓	✓		✓			
5:55 PM	USHERS SEAT BRIDE'S MOTHER		✓									✓			
5:55 PM	ATTENDANTS LINE UP FOR PROCESSION				✓	✓						✓		✓	✓
5:56 PM	BRIDE'S FATHER TAKES HIS PLACE NEXT TO BRIDE	✓		✓											
5:57 PM	USHERS ROLL OUT AISLE RUNNER											✓			
5:58 PM	GROOM'S PARTY ENTERS							✓			✓				
6:00 PM	PROCESSIONAL MUSIC BEGINS														

WEDDING PARTY TIMELINE (SAMPLE)

This is a sample timeline.
Create your own timeline on the following pages.

TIME	DESCRIPTION	BRIDE	BRIDE'S MOTHER	BRIDE'S FATHER	MAID OF HONOR	BRIDESMAIDS	BRIDE'S FAMILY	GROOM	GROOM'S MOTHER	GROOM'S FATHER	BEST MAN	USHERS	GROOM'S FAMILY	FLOWER GIRL	RING BEARER
6:00 PM	GROOM'S MOTHER RISES								✓						
6:01 PM	USHERS ENTER											✓			
6:02 PM	WEDDING PARTY MARCHES UP AISLE	✓		✓	✓	✓								✓	✓
6:20 PM	WEDDING PARTY MARCHES DOWN AISLE	✓			✓			✓			✓			✓	✓
6:22 PM	PARENTS MARCH DOWN AISLE		✓	✓					✓	✓					
6:25 PM	SIGN MARRIAGE CERTIFICATE	✓			✓			✓			✓				
6:30 PM	POST-CEREMONY PHOTOS TAKEN	✓	✓	✓	✓	✓	✓	✓	✓	✓	✓	✓	✓	✓	✓
6:30 PM	COCKTAILS AND HORS D'OEUVRES SERVED														
6:30 PM	GIFT ATTENDANT WATCHES GIFTS AS GUESTS ARRIVE														
7:15 PM	BAND/DJ ANNOUNCES ENTRANCE AND/ OR RECEIVING LINE FORMS	✓						✓							
7:45 PM	GUESTS ARE SEATED AND DINNER IS SERVED														
8:30 PM	TOASTS ARE GIVEN										✓				
8:40 PM	FIRST DANCE	✓						✓							
8:45 PM	TRADITIONAL DANCES	✓	✓	✓				✓	✓	✓					
9:00 PM	OPEN DANCE FLOOR FOR ALL GUESTS														
9:30 PM	BRIDE AND GROOM TOAST ONE ANOTHER BEFORE CUTTING CAKE	✓						✓							
9:40 PM	CAKE-CUTTING CEREMONY	✓						✓							
10:00 PM	BRIDE TOSSES BOUQUET TO SINGLE WOMEN	✓			✓	✓								✓	
10:10 PM	GROOM REMOVES GARTER FROM BRIDE'S LEG	✓						✓							
10:15 PM	GROOM TOSSES GARTER TO SINGLE MEN							✓			✓	✓			✓
10:20 PM	MAN WHO CAUGHT GARTER PLACES IT ON BOUQUET-CATCHING WOMAN'S LEG														
10:30 PM	DISTRIBUTE FLOWER PETALS, RICE OR BIRDSEED TO TOSS OVER COUPLE														
10:45 PM	BRIDE AND GROOM MAKE GRAND EXIT	✓						✓							

WEDDING PARTY TIMELINE

Create your own timeline using this form.
Make copies and give one to each member of your wedding party.

TIME	DESCRIPTION	BRIDE	BRIDE'S MOTHER	BRIDE'S FATHER	MAID OF HONOR	BRIDESMAIDS	BRIDE'S FAMILY	GROOM	GROOM'S MOTHER	GROOM'S FATHER	BEST MAN	USHERS	GROOM'S FAMILY	FLOWER GIRL	RING BEARER

WEDDING PARTY TIMELINE

Create your own timeline using this form.
Make copies and give one to each member of your wedding party.

TIME	DESCRIPTION	BRIDE	BRIDE'S MOTHER	BRIDE'S FATHER	MAID OF HONOR	BRIDESMAIDS	BRIDE'S FAMILY	GROOM	GROOM'S MOTHER	GROOM'S FATHER	BEST MAN	USHERS	GROOM'S FAMILY	FLOWER GIRL	RING BEARER

This is a sample timeline.
Create your own timeline on the following pages.

TIME	DESCRIPTION	BAKERY	CATERER	CEREMONY MUSICIANS	OFFICIANT	OTHER	FLORIST	HAIRSTYLIST	LIMOUSINE	MAKEUP ARTIST	MANICURIST	PARTY RENTALS	PHOTOGRAPHER	RECEPTION MUSICIANS	VIDEOGRAPHER
1:00 PM	PARTY RENTAL SUPPLIER DELIVERS SUPPLIES TO CEREMONY SITE											✓			
1:30 PM	PARTY RENTAL SUPPLIER DELIVERS SUPPLIES TO RECEPTION SITE											✓			
2:00 PM	MANICURIST MEETS BRIDE AT:										✓				
2:30 PM	MAKEUP ARTIST MEETS BRIDE AT:									✓					
3:00 PM	HAIRSTYLIST MEETS BRIDE AT:							✓							
4:00 PM	LIMOUSINE PICKS UP BRIDAL PARTY AT:								✓						
4:15 PM	CATERER BEGINS SETTING UP		✓												
4:30 PM	FLORIST ARRIVES AT CEREMONY SITE						✓								
4:40 PM	BAKER DELIVERS CAKE TO RECEPTION SITE	✓													
4:45 PM	FLORIST ARRIVES AT RECEPTION SITE						✓								
4:45 PM	PRE-CEREMONY PHOTOS OF GROOM'S FAMILY AT:												✓		
5:00 PM	VIDEOGRAPHER ARRIVES AT CEREMONY SITE														✓
5:15 PM	PRE-CEREMONY PHOTOS OF BRIDE'S FAMILY AT:												✓		
5:20 PM	CEREMONY SITE DECORATIONS FINALIZED (GUEST BOOK, FLOWERS, ETC.)					✓	✓								
5:30 PM	PRELUDE MUSIC BEGINS			✓											
5:45 PM	RECEPTION SITE DECORATIONS FINALIZED (GIFT TABLE, PLACE CARDS, ETC.)		✓			✓	✓								
5:58 PM	OFFICIANT ENTERS				✓										
6:00 PM	PROCESSIONAL MUSIC BEGINS			✓											
6:15 PM	CATERER FINISHES SETTING UP		✓												
6:25 PM	SIGN MARRIAGE CERTIFICATE				✓								✓		✓
6:30 PM	POST-CEREMONY PHOTOS AT:												✓		
6:30 PM	COCKTAILS AND HORS D'OEUVRES SERVED		✓												
6:30 PM	BAND OR DJ BEGINS PLAYING													✓	

SERVICE PROVIDER TIMELINE (SAMPLE)

This is a sample timeline.
Create your own timeline on the following pages.

TIME	DESCRIPTION	BAKERY	CATERER	CEREMONY MUSICIANS	OFFICIANT	OTHER	FLORIST	HAIRSTYLIST	LIMOUSINE	MAKEUP ARTIST	MANICURIST	PARTY RENTALS	PHOTOGRAPHER	RECEPTION MUSICIANS	VIDEOGRAPHER
6:30 PM	TRANSPORT GUEST BOOK AND GIFTS TO RECEPTION SITE					✓									
6:45 PM	MOVE ARCH/URNS/FLOWERS TO RECEPTION SITE					✓									
7:00 PM	LIMOUSINE PICKS UP BRIDE AND GROOM AT CEREMONY SITE								✓						
7:15 PM	BAND/DJ ANNOUNCES ENTRANCE OF BRIDE AND GROOM													✓	
7:45 PM	DINNER IS SERVED		✓												
8:15 PM	CHAMPAGNE SERVED FOR TOASTS		✓												
8:30 PM	BAND/DJ ANNOUNCES TOAST BY BEST MAN													✓	
8:40 PM	BAND/DJ ANNOUNCES FIRST DANCE													✓	
9:00 PM	TRANSPORT GIFTS TO:					✓									
9:30 PM	BAND/DJ ANNOUNCES CAKE-CUTTING CEREMONY													✓	
10:30 PM	TRANSPORT TOP TIER OF CAKE, CAKE-TOP, FLOWERS, ETC. TO:					✓									
10:40 PM	TRANSPORT RENTAL ITEMS TO:					✓									
10:45 PM	LIMOUSINE PICKS UP BRIDE AND GROOM AT RECEPTION SITE								✓						
11:00 PM	VIDEOGRAPHER DEPARTS														✓
11:00 PM	PHOTOGRAPHER DEPARTS												✓		
11:00 PM	WEDDING CONSULTANT DEPARTS					✓									
11:30 PM	BAND/DJ STOPS PLAYING													✓	
11:45 PM	PARTY RENTAL SUPPLIER PICKS UP SUPPLIES AT CEREMONY/RECEPTION SITES											✓			

SERVICE PROVIDER TIMELINE

Create your own timeline using this form.
Make copies and give one to each of your service providers.

TIME	DESCRIPTION	BAKERY	CATERER	CEREMONY MUSICIANS	OFFICIANT	OTHER	FLORIST	HAIRSTYLIST	LIMOUSINE	MAKEUP ARTIST	MANICURIST	PARTY RENTALS	PHOTOGRAPHER	RECEPTION MUSICIANS	VIDEOGRAPHER

SERVICE PROVIDER TIMELINE

Create your own timeline using this form.
Make copies and give one to each of your service providers.

TIME	DESCRIPTION	BAKERY	CATERER	CEREMONY MUSICIANS	OFFICIANT	OTHER	FLORIST	HAIRSTYLIST	LIMOUSINE	MAKEUP ARTIST	MANICURIST	PARTY RENTALS	PHOTOGRAPHER	RECEPTION MUSICIANS	VIDEOGRAPHER

WEDDING PLANNING CALENDAR

Month:_____ 20_____ Number of months before wedding:_____

SUNDAY	MONDAY	TUESDAY	WEDNESDAY	THURSDAY	FRIDAY	SATURDAY

Notes:_____
_____

WEDDING PLANNING CALENDAR

Month:_____   20_____   Number of months before wedding:_____

SUNDAY	MONDAY	TUESDAY	WEDNESDAY	THURSDAY	FRIDAY	SATURDAY

Notes:_____

_____

WEDDING PLANNING CALENDAR

Month:_____   20_____   Number of months before wedding:_____

SUNDAY	MONDAY	TUESDAY	WEDNESDAY	THURSDAY	FRIDAY	SATURDAY

Notes:_____

_____

WEDDING PLANNING CALENDAR

Month:_____   20_____   Number of months before wedding:_____

SUNDAY	MONDAY	TUESDAY	WEDNESDAY	THURSDAY	FRIDAY	SATURDAY

Notes:_____

WEDDING PLANNING CALENDAR

Month:_____   __20_____   Number of months before wedding:_____

SUNDAY	MONDAY	TUESDAY	WEDNESDAY	THURSDAY	FRIDAY	SATURDAY

Notes:_____

_____

WEDDING PLANNING CALENDAR

Month:_____   20_____   Number of months before wedding:_____

SUNDAY	MONDAY	TUESDAY	WEDNESDAY	THURSDAY	FRIDAY	SATURDAY

Notes:_____

_____

WEDDING PLANNING CALENDAR

Month:_____ 20_____ Number of months before wedding:_____

SUNDAY	MONDAY	TUESDAY	WEDNESDAY	THURSDAY	FRIDAY	SATURDAY

Notes:_____

WEDDING PLANNING CALENDAR

Month:_____   20_____   Number of months before wedding:_____

SUNDAY	MONDAY	TUESDAY	WEDNESDAY	THURSDAY	FRIDAY	SATURDAY

Notes:_____

_____

WEDDING PLANNING CALENDAR

Month:_____   20___   Number of months before wedding:_____

SUNDAY	MONDAY	TUESDAY	WEDNESDAY	THURSDAY	FRIDAY	SATURDAY

Notes:_____

WEDDING PLANNING CALENDAR

Month:_____   20_____   Number of months before wedding:_____

SUNDAY	MONDAY	TUESDAY	WEDNESDAY	THURSDAY	FRIDAY	SATURDAY

Notes:_____

_____

WEDDING PLANNING CALENDAR

Month:_____   20_____   Number of months before wedding:_____

SUNDAY	MONDAY	TUESDAY	WEDNESDAY	THURSDAY	FRIDAY	SATURDAY

Notes:_____

WEDDING PLANNING CALENDAR

Month:_____ 20_____ Number of months before wedding:_____

SUNDAY	MONDAY	TUESDAY	WEDNESDAY	THURSDAY	FRIDAY	SATURDAY

Notes:_____

_____

WeddingSolutions.com

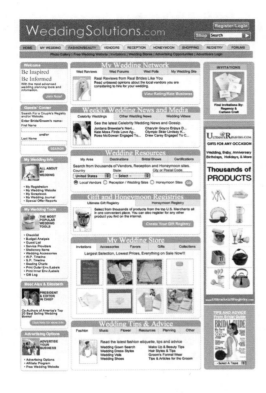

Everything You Need to Plan Your Dream Wedding

- The Latest Wedding Gowns
- Comprehensive Wedding Planning Tools
- Articles, Tips & Advice
- Thousands of Local Vendors
- Beautiful Reception Sites
- Honeymoon Destinations
- Largest Online Wedding Store
- Wedding Forums
- Personal Wedding Website
- Honeymoon & Gift Registry
- Polls, News, Videos, Media
- Wedding Planning Certification Programs

SEARCH FOR WEDDING GOWNS
View the Latest Designs

Search for your perfect wedding gown by designer, style and price.

SEARCH FOR RESOURCES
Reputable & Reliable

Find local vendors, reception, honeymoon & destination wedding sites.

Log on to www.WeddingSolutions.com for more information

WeddingSolutions.com

$99 Value

FREE Wedding Website
on WeddingSolutions.com

Includes 19 Custom Pages

- Home
- Our Story
- Photo Gallery
- Details of Events
- Wedding Party
- Registry
- Local Info
- City Guide
- Accommodations
- Things to Do

- Restaurants
- Guest Book
- View Guest Book
- Sign Guest Book
- Wedding Journal
- Honeymoon
- Miscellaneous
- RSVP
- Contact Us
- Much More

SAVE UP TO $200 ON WEDDING INVITATIONS & ACCESSORIES

Invitations..........................

SAVE up to $100

- Wedding Invitations
- Engagement
- Bridal Shower
- Rehearsal Dinner
- Casual Wedding
- Seal 'n Send
- Save The Date
- Maps/Direction Cards
- Programs
- Thank-You Notes
- Much More!

Accessories..........................

SAVE up to $100

- Toasting Glasses
- Attendants' Gifts
- Unity Candles
- Aisle Runners
- Cake Tops
- Flower Girl Basket
- Ring Pillow
- Guest Book
- Cake Knife & Server
- Favors
- Much More!

Log on to www.WeddingSolutions.com/specialxoffers
for more details on these offers

WedSpace.com

THE BEST WAY TO PLAN YOUR ENTIRE WEDDING!

‹ Wedding Journal
Share your Love Story: All about you and your partner, how you met and got engaged. Upload photos and videos, inform your guests on pre-wedding parties, where to stay, local info, and more.

‹ Photo Slideshow
Share your photos with friends and family!

‹ Create a Network
Engaged couples, wedding guests, wedding vendors, family and friends

‹ Wedding Wall
Share, connect and discover! Exchange ideas and view photos and videos. Chat with vendors, get advice from real brides and much more.

Guests Can Meet
Your wedding guests can chat and share media before, during, and after the wedding.

Facebook Connect
You can easily transfer your Facebook friends, wall, and photos to WedSpace and invite your friends to view your journal.

Log on to WedSpace.com to create your FREE Wedding Journal today!

WedSpace.com

FREE Online Wedding Journal!
$29.95 Value

A fun and exciting way to share your Love Story
and Wedding Details with friends and family.

Celebrating the Wedding of
Chelsea & Trever
June 10th, 2011 • 348 days to go!

Friend Request Send to Friend Send Message Send E-Card Invite to Group Add to Favorites

HOME   OUR STORY   WEDDING DETAILS   REGISTRY   RSVP   MEDIA   VIEW OUR

Welcome to our Wedding Journal!
To read our love story, view our wedding details, see where we have registered, RSVP
and so much more, simply log in or register and click on "Friend Request." You will be
able to read our Wedding Wall/blog, meet our wedding vendors and other guests who are
coming to the wedding, and so much more.

Answer quick questions and upload photos and videos to customize
pages including:

- All About Him
- All About Her
- How We Met

- Our Engagement
- Ceremony Details
- Reception Details

- Where to Stay
- And much more

The perfect tool for your guests to RSVP for your wedding and find out where you have registered!

Create Your FREE Online Wedding Journal Today!
(Use discount code "FREE3369" during registration)